# תַּדְרִיךְ לְשַׁבָּת

# A SHABBAT MANUAL

Published for
THE CENTRAL CONFERENCE OF AMERICAN RABBIS
by
KTAV PUBLISHING HOUSE, INC.
1972

SBN 87068-199-0

ı

MANUFACTURED IN THE UNITED STATES OF AMERICA
LIBRARY OF CONGRESS CATALOG CARD NUMBER: 72-10299

# EDITOR'S INTRODUCTION

This Manual represents an effort on the part of the Central Conference of American Rabbis to create old/new opportunities for Jewish living. It is also a major attempt of the Reform rabbinate to deal directly with Reform Halachah in specific form, with guidelines responsive to the needs and realities of Diaspora life.

In 1965 the Conference commissioned a newly created Sabbath Committee to study the possibilities of revitalizing Shabbat as the central institution of Jewish life. In the course of years the following rabbis have served on the Committee: Frederic A. Doppelt ז״ל, Herbert M. Baumgard, Henry E. Kagan ז״ל, Robert I. Kahn, Joseph Klein, Joseph Narot, Herbert H. Rose and Herman E. Schaalman. Out of many seminars, surveys, meetings and pilot studies which involved a series of congregations, came the suggestion to create a Manual which would bring to Jewish homes as well as individuals a tool for celebrating Shabbat in the spirit of our times. In 1969, at its Houston convention, the Conference adopted the Manual (which had been submitted to the entire membership for critical comment) and asked KTAV Publishing House, Inc. to undertake its publication.

Acknowledgment is made to Mr. John Colombo for his editorial assistance, and to Rabbis Sidney L. Regner, Joseph B. Glaser, and Malcolm Stern for helping to bring this book into print. We are particularly grateful to Mr. Bernard Scharfstein of KTAV for his concerned participation in this joint enterprise, which we now lay before you in the hope that you will study it and from study proceed to doing.

*W. Gunther Plaut,*
Chairman, Sabbath Committee

III

# CONTENTS

# SHABBAT OBSERVANCE

# PREFACE

This is a book about Shabbat. We know that Shabbat, as a discipline and as a source of noble living, has been lost to large numbers of our people, a loss which is both tragic and unnecessary. This Manual is our beginning in the effort to recover Shabbat observance as an enhancement of Jewish life, both for the individual Jew and for our people as a whole.

Jews who have discarded Shabbat observance or Jews who have been deprived of it will not find it easy to reclaim all its treasures for themselves and their children. This Manual is a guide to these treasures. It is yours to use.

We can only begin where we are. Each individual and each family will decide where and how to begin, and what and how much to do to make Shabbat an essential element in the rhythm of life. Our shared faith in God, our love of the Jewish people, and our devotion to the Torah tradition give us a common base from which to start. The use of the following pages now depends on you.

# SHABBAT IN OUR DAY

The advent of Emancipation toward the end of the eighteenth century and the slow but steady stream of Jews into the Western world produced profound changes in Jewish religious habits. As long as Jews lived within the autonomous confines of the ghetto or the Jewish quarter, their community was clearly defined, and the authority of Jewish leaders and Jewish law remained strong. As Jews began to adapt themselves to the economic and social patterns of the environment, many of the mainstays of tradition began to weaken and eventually gave way.

One of these was Shabbat. In the past, the Jew had lived primarily with his own people, and the fact that the rest of the world did not observe his Shabbat was of little concern to him. But since the onset of Emancipation, the Shabbat, along with many other Jewish institutions, has had to fight a rear-guard battle.

People began to work on Shabbat in order to secure the necessities for living. With increasing urbanization, the problem of transportation began to arise. Jews began to question the authority of the rabbis and, with the rise of biblical criticism, the authority of the biblical word itself. They understood that the Bible was not in fact the direct word of God but was, in its present form, essentially a human document which had to be humanly interpreted—even though the belief remained strong that God had something to do with Bible and tradition. But no longer could the old theory be maintained that rabbinic interpretation of biblical law was the only valid realization of God's word in human life. Change became the password of the modern age, and everything, including religion, was subject to it.

With change came the deterioration of many aspects of tradition, especially an attenuation of public and private worship, and a lessening of personal religious practices. The stubborn refusal of old-line Jewish authorities to come to grips with the pressing questions raised by a totally new age brought the Reform movement into being. In turn, its rise further hardened the opposition, so that toward the middle of the nineteenth century Jewish life in Western Europe was divided between traditionalists and reformers. In time the reformers themselves split into a liberal wing and a more conservative wing. Toward the beginning of the twentieth century, the latter formed a separate movement called Conservatism.

2

From its beginning, Reform tried desperately to shore up the Shabbat as a pillar of Jewish existence. The literature of the past hundred years is replete with attempts made in this direction by rabbis and congregations. They tried to persuade business men to keep their establishments closed; they tried to define the limits of permissible labor, and they valiantly struggled to save the precious heritage of weekly worship. Having failed and believing that Shabbat itself was probably lost, some tried to save "the spirit of Shabbat" by shifting the main weekly services to Sunday, in order to rescue at least the worship service from the crumbling Shabbat edifice. In vain . . . by 1933, there seemed little likelihood that the trend toward further weakening and dissolution of the old Shabbat could be halted—even by the most radical of means.

But events since that time—virulent Naziism, the destruction of European Jewry, the rise of the State of Israel—once again profoundly altered the thought-patterns of Jewry. A sense of peoplehood and personal obligation came much to the fore, a new sense that mitzvah was a necessary component of Jewish life became stronger among many Jews, even those far removed from tradition. Vast changes in economic circumstances made new developments possible. Urbanization and the corollary erosion of personal identity, on the one hand, and the increase of leisure time, on the other, made it necessary to revise old ideas of rest and suggested the possibility of new Shabbat observances. Other novel factors included a generally greater identification with institutional religion and a dramatic increase of the older and retired portions of the population who could and would give added personal commitment to the synagogues. All these and other factors presented new challenges to, and opportunities for, Jewish life.

The very nature and concept of "work" were changing. The spread of the five-day week, even the four-day week, altered the structure of Western civilization. Young people were spending added years in study, many aspects of which would formerly have qualified as labor. For older people, leisure often became a burden and "work" a relief from it, thereby reversing the traditional order of desirability Little remained of former foundations; much was in transition.

In 1965, the Central Conference of American Rabbis resolved to make a concerted effort to utilize the potential of these developments toward a revitalization of Shabbat. This Manual is a part of this resolve, but the realization of the potential must lie with the individual Jew. By precept and example, rabbis may speak of Shabbat and urge their congregants to love, remember, and observe it. It is the Jewish individual and the Jewish family who will be the builders of Shabbat, and thereby the builders of a rejuvenated Jewish edifice.

Among large numbers of our people only a few negative Shabbat commands are still observed. We do not have funerals or weddings on the seventh day, but otherwise there are more exceptions than observances. Of the positive commands, equally little remains, like the lighting of the candles, a simple Kiddush, and an occasional visit to the synagogue. Beyond these remnants must lie a renewed commitment of the Jew to his people and to his future and, in a deeper sense, a commitment also to the God of Israel. Since we can no longer make this commitment under the force of communal disapproval or penalty, we must make it by free decision. We must do it because this is how we *want* to live, and because we know that this is how we ought to live. Here the concept of mitzvah enters.

Earlier generations understood mitzvah in a literal sense, as though a particular observance were willed in every detail by God Himself. For us, mitzvah means that God offers an opportunity to introduce an "ought" into our existence. To accept this opportunity and act on it is not easy; it demands self-discipline. The reward is in accordance with the effort: "The reward of doing a mitzvah is to be able to do further mitzvot."

# PURPOSES OF SHABBAT OBSERVANCE

What we do or abstain from doing on Shabbat should be directed toward the fulfillment of five major purposes. These five purposes historically have been identified with Shabbat and represent the core of Jewish existence as expressed in "Shemirat Shabbat," Sabbath observance.

### 1. *Awareness of the World.*

In our weekday life, we rarely pause to consider the nature of the universe around us; we seldom meditate on the meaning and purpose of our existence in it. The observance of Shabbat affords us a singular opportunity to reflect upon the marvel of the universe which God has created, to rejoice in the glory and beauty of creation, and to consider our part in God's continuing process of creation. This is the core of the Fourth Commandment (in Exodus), and is emphasized in the Kiddush which reminds us that the Shabbat is instituted "in remembrance of the work of creation" (Zikaron Lema'aseh Bereshit).

### 2. *Commitment to Freedom.*

In our tradition, God is acknowledged not only as a creator and source of life but also as a presence in human history, especially in the history of the Jewish people. The Kiddush also speaks of Shabbat as "a memorial of the exodus from Egypt" (Zecher Litzi'at Mitzrayim, reflecting the Fourth Commandment in Deuteronomy). This means that as God delivered us from slavery so must we strive to help all who suffer from every form of bondage and degradation in the world. Shabbat reminds us of our historic commitment to freedom and justice. It shows us the world that can be if we will it.

### 3. *Identity with the Jewish People.*

On Shabbat, we have a weekly opportunity to remember God's covenant (Berit) with Israel and to reaffirm our identity with, and loyalty to, the house of Israel. Shabbat is "a sign between Me and the children of Israel forever." It summons us to a renewal of our responsibility to promote the welfare and dignity of the Jewish people. It calls upon each Jew to help further the high and noble purposes of the community and to use the precious hours of the Shabbat to deepen the unique historic fellowship of the Jewish people.

## 4. *Enhancement of the Person.*

The Shabbat tradition provides three modes for the enhancement of personal life: Kedushah, Menuchah, Oneg.

Kedushah (holiness) requires that Shabbat be singled out as different from the weekdays. It must be distinguished from the other days of the week so that those who observe it will become transformed by its holiness. One ought, therefore, to do certain things which contribute to an awareness of this day's special nature, and to abstain from doing others which lessen our awareness.

Menuchah (rest), as expressed through Shabbat, is more than relaxation and abstention from work. It is a condition of the soul, a physical and spiritual release from weekday pressures. If the week is characterized by competition, rush, and turmoil, their absence will contribute to serenity. It is this quality of Menuchah which leads tradition to call Shabbat "a foretaste of the days of the Messiah."

Oneg (joy), as experienced on Shabbat, is more than fun and pleasure. It is the kind of joy that enhances our personal lives and leaves us truly enriched for the week ahead. Shabbat gives us a quantity of "free" time and, thereby, a qualitative potential of freedom—time during which man can be himself and do for himself and for others what he could never accomplish during the other days of the week.

## 5. *Dedication to Peace.*

More than any other day, Shabbat embodies our yearning for peace. Its traditional greeting, "Shabbat Shalom," as well as the day's all-pervasive mood, attunes us to the value of peace and teaches its centrality in the Jew's hope for the world today and for the future. Each week it calls us to renewed effort and dedication "to make peace between man and man." Shabbat can become a foundation of human reconciliation, for as we observe it and remember its purposes, we—and thereby the world—will have made a turning toward peace.

The rewards of making Shabbat meaningful are many. We cannot afford to spurn them. As Jews, we ought to know that Shabbat is one of the cornerstones of our faith. When we secure this cornerstone for ourselves, we do so for the kingdom of God and for the community of the Eternal People.

# GUIDELINES TO SHABBAT MITZVOT

*What Is a Mitzvah?*

Mitzvah (plural, mitzvot) is what a Jew ought to do in response
to his God and to the tradition of his people. This response comes
from personal commitment rather than from unquestioning obedi-
ence to a set of commandments which past tradition thought to be
the direct will of God. By making choice and commitment part
of our plan of life, we willingly and purposefully strengthen our
bonds with the God of Israel and with His people.

Mitzvah is, therefore, more than folkway and ceremony. As
we choose to do a mitzvah—be it a positive act or a negative act
(an abstention)—we choose the way of duty, of self-discipline,
and of loyalty. To do so with eagerness and joy is the true seal of
Shabbat observance.

This Manual lists Shabbat Mitzvot and offers options and opportunities. It is suggested that you make a permanent decision to
apply the principles of this catalogue of mitzvot to your life. You
may do this for yourself alone, or together with your family, or
as a member of a group of like-minded Jews who seek such a
commitment. The practices of your community may, of course,
bear on the extent or nature of your own performance.*

In making a decision, you may wish to be guided by historical
considerations and rabbinical responses to specific problems. These
and other matters may be found later in this Manual. It is important to remember that Shabbat and its opportunities last for
twenty-four hours, from sunset to sunset.

*How Much Ought I Observe?*

To make Shabbat meaningful, observe as much as you can. Begin
from where you are now, with what you presently do or do not do.
If your Shabbat is like a weekday, begin with any mitzvah, but
begin. Make your decision into a habit. From a modest start you
may progress to a more significant observance. If you presently

---

*This Manual makes no attempt to speak specifically to the unique situ-
ation of Jews who live in the State of Israel.

observe some mitzvot, search for the opportunity to deepen or enlarge that practice.*

You must always remember that you are performing mitzvot. It is not a question of "how you feel about it" at any given time. You may not be "in the mood." But being a Jew is not always convenient or easy. The performance of mitzvot ought to be the pattern of one's life. The more deep-rooted such a pattern, the more intense and regular one's performance of mitzvot, the richer and truer will be one's life as a Jew. Do not become discouraged because the Manual contains mitzvot which you cannot now fulfill. The secret of observing a mitzvah is to begin. And as we begin, one or several of the five purposes of Shabbat observance will be fulfilled in our lives.

---

*When in doubt about any item or phase of Shabbat observance, consult your rabbi. Further details may also be found below, pp. 92-100.

# CATALOGUE OF SHABBAT OPPORTUNITIES
## What to Do (Mitzvot Aseh)

On Erev Shabbat (Friday)

*1. It is a mitzvah for the family to prepare for Shabbat and to celebrate it together.*

Special Shabbat preparations include: cleaning the house; flowers or decoration in the dining room; setting a festive table; appropriate dress; inviting a Shabbat guest for dinner. If the head of the household and/or members of the family have to work late, the meal, if possible, should be delayed until all can gather.

*2. It is a mitzvah to light Shabbat candles with the appropriate blessing.*

The lighting of the candles in the synagogue is no substitute for the performance of the mitzvah of lighting Shabbat candles in the home.

*3. It is a mitzvah to recite or chant the Kiddush.*

It is customary for all present to drink Kiddush wine after the head of the household or his substitute has completed the recitation of the Kiddush. Some provide Kiddush cups for each child over bar and bat mitzvah or confirmation age. The recitation of the Kiddush in the synagogue is no substitute for the performance of the mitzvah of Kiddush in the home.

*4. It is a mitzvah to recite or chant the Motzi before, and the Birkat Hamazon after, the meal.*

Motzi is said over the challah, a piece of which afterwards is eaten by all present. It is a hallowed custom for the parents to bless their children, grown-up or young, on Shabbat and holy days. In many homes, the head of the household recites "A Woman of Valor," while children in turn ask God's blessing on their elders. A festive meal should be eaten on Shabbat

9

evening. It is customary to sing Zemirot (Sabbath Hymns) and to talk about subjects appropriate to the day. This is also an ideal opportunity for sharing those matters which give all members of the family, young and old, a sense of common purpose. It is customary to invite members of the household and guests to participate in the Birkat Hamazon which is ended by wishing each other "Shabbat Shalom" or "Good Shabbos."

5. *It is a mitzvah to join the Congregation in worship.*

All members of the family, except small children, should attend services together whether they are held at sundown or later in the evening. If illness, emergency, preparations for the Shabbat, or other unavoidable circumstances prevent synagogue attendance, Shabbat evening prayers should be said in the home. After fulfilling the mitzvah of worship, it is customary to visit with relatives and friends, or engage in such other activities as will enhance Oneg Shabbat, the joy of the Sabbath.

## On Shabbat Day

The mitzvot of the day are based upon the traditional principles of Torah (study), Avodah (worship), and Gemilut Chasadim (acts of social concern).

6. *It is a mitzvah to join the congregation in worship.*

All members of the family, except small children, should attend services together. School-age children and young people may also attend religious school.

While the mitzvah of Talmud Torah (study of Torah) applies to everyday, it has special relevance for Shabbat. The reading from the Sidra (weekly Torah selection) during services is one of its high points. It should lead to further appropriate reading and related study, which will be enhanced immeasurably when members of the family share such Shabbat activity with each other. Where illness, emergency or other unavoidable circumstances prevent synagogue attendance, Shabbat prayers are said in the home. Selections from the weekly Sidra should also be read. It is customary to recite or chant the Kiddush following the morning prayers. The recitation of the Kiddush in the synagogue is no substitute for the performance of the mitzvah in the home.

*7. It is a mitzvah to maintain and enjoy the special quality of Shabbat throughout the afternoon.*

This may be done by choosing from among those opportunities which will complement and enrich one's particular life style. Among these are: rest; visit to friends; visit to shut-ins or the sick; engaging in Jewish or general communal activities which promote the welfare of the community; cultural activities. Special care should be taken to conduct oneself in such a manner and to participate in such activities as will enhance the distinctive Shabbat qualities of Kedushah, Menuchah, and Oneg.

*8. It is a mitzvah to recite Havdalah.*

To perform the mitzvah of Havdalah at sundown or later, one uses the special Havdalah candle, the besameem (spices in a box), and a cup filled with wine, and one recites or chants the appropriate blessings over them. It is customary for the youngest person present to hold the Havdalah candle and for all present to participate in singing Havdalah Zemirot. It is a hallowed custom for parents to bless their children, grown-up or young, at the end of Shabbat.

The synagogue and its facilities should be available during the entire Shabbat day for worship, study, and fellowship, and it should maintain a full schedule of religious services, Torah reading, study, and such other activities as will promote the distinctive Shabbat qualities of Kedushah, Menuchah, and Oneg.

## What Not to Do (Mitzvot Lo Ta'aseh)

Shemirat Shabbat requires not only positive mitzvot (mitzvot aseh), but also negative mitzvot (mitzvot lo ta'aseh). Affirmations inevitably entail abstentions and renunciations. The Shabbat is truly celebrated and enjoyed both by doing and by not doing. We do those things which express and affirm the spirit and the values of Shabbat. We refrain from doing those things which contradict the spirit and the values of Shabbat. Following is a suggested list of things-not-to-do on the Shabbat. It sets down general principles but does not go into great detail. It does not, for instance, classify sports or recreational activities beyond what is stated in

#14. Experience and personal circumstance will indicate whether these and other activities (such as gardening) are to be classed as competitive and/or as work and therefore to be avoided, or as rest in the sense of Menuchah. (See further details below, pp. 98-100.)

9. *It is a mitzvah not to engage in gainful work on Shabbat.*
Abstinence from gainful work is a major goal of Shabbat observance. Where compelling economic circumstances require an individual to perform gainful work on Shabbat, he should nevertheless bear this goal in mind and should perform as many positive Shabbat mitzvot as possible. All unnecessary or occasional business transactions should be postponed until after Shabbat.

10. *It is a mitzvah not to perform housework on Shabbat.*
No heavy work is to be done in the home or on its outside premises except for emergency and unavoidable preparation of food. This applies from sunset to sunset to all members of the household and to its employees.

11. *It is a mitzvah to refrain from shopping on Shabbat.*
This mitzvah should be set aside only for an emergency.

12. *It is mitzvah not to participate in a social event during Shabbat worship hours.*
To perform this mitzvah, one must not schedule a social event at a time which conflicts with the Shabbat worship hours set by the congregation, nor attend social events scheduled for that time. Jewish organizations are equally obligated to observe this mitzvah.

13. *It is a mitzvah not to schedule or participate in a public event during Shabbat worship hours.*
Jewish organizations are obligated to observe this mitzvah and not schedule any public, cultural, or other event during Shabbat worship hours. It may become necessary to object to civic functions which conflict with Shabbat worship hours and to refuse participation in them. Young people are subject to complex pressures of their own. Nonetheless, Shemirat Shabbat is an obligation also for them, and the young should not attend public functions which conflict with Shabbat worship hours,

whether sponsored by the school or other public bodies. Youth services may be rescheduled so as to avoid conflict in this area.

*14. It is a mitzvah to avoid all public activity which violates or gives the appearance of violating Shemirat Shabbat.*

Care should be taken that our conduct and participation in public activities shall avoid giving offence to other Jews. We should enhance the distinctive Shabbat qualities of Kedushah, Menuchah, and Oneg and not violate them. Athletics, hobbies, and other leisure activities should not be pursued during Shabbat worship hours. Wedding ceremonies, which are in fact also legal transactions, may not be conducted before sunset on Saturday. In making unavoidable final preparations for weddings, care should be taken to preserve the spirit of Shabbat. No funerals are held on Shabbat, nor ought one to visit the cemetery. The mitzvah of comforting the mourners by visiting them may be performed during Shabbat, except during worship hours. Construction work or maintenance which can be done on other days may not be performed in the synagogue or Jewish communal building on the Shabbat. This applies to all workmen, regardless of their religion. Many synagogues discourage smoking on their premises during Shabbat.

In the performance of the mitzvot of Shemirat Shabbat, our teaching and example count most heavily. The family ought to remain together during Shabbat and share as many Shabbat activities as possible. Its Shabbat life should rest upon the traditional foundation of all Jewish life: Torah, Avodah, and Gemilut Chasadim.

As Israel preserves the Shabbat, so the Shabbat preserves Israel.

# HOME SERVICES

## הַדְלָקַת הַנֵּר — Lighting the Candles

*The mother—or, in her absence, a daughter or other member of the household—lights the candles and recites the prayers. Single persons should also observe the mitzvah.*

The Lord is our light and our salvation. In His name we kindle these Shabbat lights. May they bring into our household the beauty of truth and the radiance of love's understanding. On this Shabbat eve, and at all times, "Let there be light."

Be praised, Lord our God, King of the universe, who has sanctified us by His laws and given us the mitzvah of kindling the Shabbat light.

בָּרוּךְ אַתָּה יְיָ, אֱלֹהֵינוּ מֶלֶךְ הָעוֹלָם,
אֲשֶׁר קִדְּשָׁנוּ בְּמִצְוֹתָיו וְצִוָּנוּ
לְהַדְלִיק נֵר שֶׁל שַׁבָּת.

May the Lord bless us with Shabbat joy.
May the Lord bless us with Shabbat holiness.
May the Lord bless us with Shabbat peace.

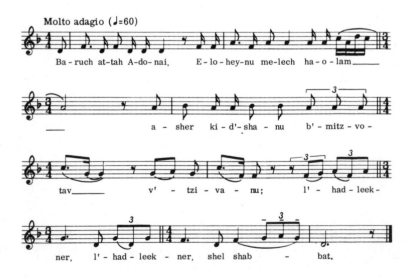

16

# קִדּוּשׁ לְלֵיל שַׁבָּת — Shabbat Eve Kiddush

*It is customary to use wine in a special cup. Where no wine is available, bread may be used, and the motzi should then be substituted for the first blessing. Thereafter, the remainder of the Kiddush should be said. The father says the blessings; in his absence, a son or anyone else could say them. Single persons should also observe the mitzvah.*

בָּרוּךְ אַתָּה יְיָ,
אֱלֹהֵינוּ מֶלֶךְ הָעוֹלָם,
בּוֹרֵא פְּרִי הַגָּפֶן.

Be praised, O Lord, our God,
Ruler of the Universe,
Creator of the fruit of the vine.

בָּרוּךְ אַתָּה יְיָ,
אֱלֹהֵינוּ מֶלֶךְ הָעוֹלָם,
אֲשֶׁר קִדְּשָׁנוּ בְּמִצְוֹתָיו
וְרָצָה בָנוּ.

Be praised, O Lord, our God,
Ruler of the Universe,
Who has hallowed us
By his mitzvot and has loved
**us.**

וְשַׁבַּת קָדְשׁוֹ,
בְּאַהֲבָה וּבְרָצוֹן הִנְחִילָנוּ,
זִכָּרוֹן לְמַעֲשֵׂה בְרֵאשִׁית.

His holy Shabbat
He has lovingly and graciously
Bestowed upon us,
Recalling the act of creation.

כִּי הוּא יוֹם תְּחִלָּה
לְמִקְרָאֵי קֹדֶשׁ,
זֵכֶר לִיצִיאַת מִצְרָיִם.

It is first of the holy assemblies,
A remembrance of the going
forth from Egypt.

כִּי־בָנוּ בָחַרְתָּ,
וְאוֹתָנוּ קִדַּשְׁתָּ מִכָּל הָעַמִּים,
וְשַׁבַּת קָדְשֶׁךָ,
בְּאַהֲבָה וּבְרָצוֹן הִנְחַלְתָּנוּ:

You have chosen us and
hallowed us
From among all the peoples,
And Your holy Shabbat
You have lovingly and gra-
ciously bestowed upon us.

בָּרוּךְ אַתָּה יְיָ,
מְקַדֵּשׁ הַשַּׁבָּת:

Be praised, O Lord, who hal-
lows the Shabbat.

*Music follows →*

17

**Moderato**

Ba - ruch at-tah A - do-nai; E - lo - hey - nu me-lech ha - o -
lom, bo - rey p' - ree ha - ga - fen.

A - men. Ba -ruch at-tah A-do-nai; E-lo - hey - nu me-lech ha - o -
lom, a - sher kid' - sha - nu b'-mitz - vo - tav, v' - ra -tzah
va - nu, v'-shab-bat kod' - sho b'- a - ha-vah uv'- ra-tzon hin-chee -
la - nu, zi - ka - ron l' - ma - a - seh v're - sheet._____ Kee
hu yom t'-chi - lah, l' - mik-ra-ey ko - desh, ze - cher lee-tzee - at
mitz - ra - yim. Kee va - nu va -

char - ta v'-o - ta - nu ki - dash - ta, mi -

kol ha - a - a - meem, v'- shab - bat_____ kod -

she - cha b'- a - ha - vah uv'ra - tzon_____

hin - chal - ta - nu. Ba - ruch at - tah A - do - nai, m'-

kad - desh____ ha - shab - bat.____ A - men.

19

# הַמּוֹצִיא – The Blessing over the Bread

Gently moving

*mf*

Ha - mo - tzi le - chem min ha - a - retz, We give thanks to

God for bread; Our voic - es join in grate - ful chor - us,

*f*

As our pray'r is humb - ly said: Ba - ruch at - tah A - do -

nai, E - lo - hey - nu me - lech ha - o - lam, ha -

mo - tzi le - chem min ha - a - retz. A - men.

Be praised, Lord our God,
Ruler of the Universe, who
causes the earth to yield
food.

בָּרוּךְ אַתָּה יְיָ,
אֱלֹהֵינוּ מֶלֶךְ הָעוֹלָם,
הַמּוֹצִיא לֶחֶם מִן הָאָרֶץ.

# אֵשֶׁת־חַיִל — In Praise of Woman

*The following verses, from the Book of Proverbs 31, are said by a husband to his wife, and by children to their mother and grandmother:*

A woman of valor, who can find? for her price is far above rubies.

She looks well to the ways of her household, and does not eat the bread of idleness.

She gives food to her household, and a portion to her maidens.

She stretches out her hand to the poor; yea, she reaches forth her hands to the needy.

She opens her mouth with wisdom; and the law of kindness is on her tongue.

Strength and dignity are her clothing; and she laughs at the time to come.

Her children rise up, and call her blessed; her husband also, and he praises her: "Many daughters have done valiantly, but you excel them all."

Grace is deceitful, and beauty is vain; but a woman who fears the Lord, she shall be praised.

Give her of the fruit of her hands, and let her works praise her in the gates.

# Blessing the Children

*It is a sacred custom to bless one's children on Shabbat eve.*
*(The reference to Ephraim and Manasseh is to the blessing
Jacob gave to them; see Genesis 48.)*

יְשִׂמְךָ אֱלֹהִים כְּאֶפְרַיִם
וְכִמְנַשֶּׁה:

*To sons say:*
God make you like Ephraim and Manasseh.

יְשִׂמֵךְ אֱלֹהִים
כְּשָׂרָה רִבְקָה רָחֵל וְלֵאָה:

*To daughters say:*
God make you like Sarah, Rebekah, Rachel and Leah.

יְבָרֶכְךָ יְיָ וְיִשְׁמְרֶךָ:
יָאֵר יְיָ פָּנָיו אֵלֶיךָ וִיחֻנֶּךָּ:
יִשָּׂא יְיָ פָּנָיו אֵלֶיךָ
וְיָשֵׂם לְךָ שָׁלוֹם:

*To sons and daughters:*
The Lord bless you and keep you; the Lord make His face to shine upon you, and be gracious unto you; the Lord turn His face unto you, and give you peace.

# Blessing the Parents

*Children say these words aloud or silently:*

יְיָ יְבָרֵךְ אֶת־אַהֲבָתֵנוּ.

May God bless our love for one another.

## שַׁבַּת שָׁלוֹם — Shabbat Shalom

Shab-bat sha-lom Shab-bat sha-lom Shab-bat Shab-bat Shab-bat shab-

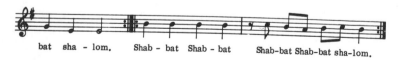

bat sha - lom. Shab - bat Shab - bat Shab-bat Shab-bat sha-lom.

## בִּרְכַּת הַמָּזוֹן – Grace after the Meal

*The Company first sing or say Psalm 126.*

שִׁיר הַמַּעֲלוֹת.

A SONG OF ASCENTS.

בְּשׁוּב יְיָ אֶת שִׁיבַת צִיּוֹן,
הָיִינוּ כְּחֹלְמִים.
אָז יִמָּלֵא
שְׂחוֹק פִּינוּ
וּלְשׁוֹנֵנוּ רִנָּה.

When the LORD brought back
those that returned to Zion,
We were like dreamers.
Then our mouths were full of
laughter,
And our tongues sang aloud
for joy.

אָז יֹאמְרוּ בַגּוֹיִם:

הִגְדִּיל יְיָ לַעֲשׂוֹת עִם אֵלֶּה.

הִגְדִּיל יְיָ לַעֲשׂוֹת עִמָּנוּ,

הָיִינוּ שְׂמֵחִים.

Then said they among the
nations:
'The LORD has done great
things for them.'
The LORD has truly done great
things for us;
We are happy.

שׁוּבָה יְיָ אֶת שְׁבִיתֵנוּ,
כַּאֲפִיקִים בַּנֶּגֶב.
הַזֹּרְעִים בְּדִמְעָה
בְּרִנָּה יִקְצֹרוּ.
הָלוֹךְ יֵלֵךְ וּבָכֹה ,
נֹשֵׂא מֶשֶׁךְ הַזָּרַע;
בֹּא יָבֹא בְרִנָּה,
נֹשֵׂא אֲלֻמֹּתָיו.

Turn our captivity, O LORD,
once again,
As streams return in the Ne-
gev.
They that sow in tears
Shall reap in joy.
Though one may bear his measure of seed and go on his
way weeping,
He shall come home in joy,
bearing his sheaves.

*Music follows →*

23

## שִׁיר הַמַּעֲלוֹת — A Song of Ascents

**Moderato**

Sheer___ ha - ma - a - lot b' - shuv___ A - do - nai
Shu - vah A - do - nai et shvee - te - nu

Et shee - vat tzee - yon ha - yee - nu k' - chol' - meem
ka - a - fee - keem___ ba - ne - gev

Az___ yi - ma - le s' - chok___ pee - nu
Ha - zor' - eem___ b' - dim - ah

u - l'-sho - ne - nu rin - nah.
b'rin - nah b'rin - nah yik - tzo - ru.

Az___ yom' - ru va - go - yeem
Ha - loch ye - lech u - va - choh

hig - deel A - do - nai la - a - sot im e - leh
no - se___ me - shech ha - za - ra;___

hig - deel A - do - nai la - a - sot im - ma - nu
bo___ ya - vo v' - rin - nah

ha - yee - nu s' - me - cheem.
no - se___ a - lu - mo - tav.

24

*Leader:*    Let us praise God.

*Company:*  May God be praised now and forever.

*Leader:*    May God be praised now and forever. Let us praise our God of whose bounty we have partaken and through His goodness we live.

*Company:*  Let us praise our God of whose bounty we have partaken and through whose goodness we live.

*Leader:*    Praised be He and praised be His name. Be praised, Lord our God, King of the universe, who sustains the world with goodness, with grace, with love and mercy. He gives food to every creature, for His mercy endures forever. Through His great goodness, we have not lacked, and may we never lack our daily bread. For God is great; He nourishes and sustains all, and deals bountifully with all, providing food for all His creatures. Be praised, O Lord, who provides food for all.

*Company:*  Sustain Jerusalem the Holy City now and ever. Be praised, Lord, who in His grace builds Jerusalem. Amen.

May He who makes peace on high, make peace for us, and for all Israel.
May God give strength to His people. May God bless His people with peace.

25

רַבּוֹתַי, נְבָרֵךְ !  *Leader*

יְהִי שֵׁם יְיָ מְבֹרָךְ  *Company*
מֵעַתָּה וְעַד עוֹלָם.

יְהִי שֵׁם יְיָ מְבֹרָךְ  *Leader*
מֵעַתָּה וְעַד עוֹלָם.
בִּרְשׁוּת מָרָנָן וְרַבּוֹתַי,
נְבָרֵךְ (אֱלֹהֵינוּ) שֶׁאָכַלְנוּ מִשֶּׁלּוֹ.

בָּרוּךְ (אֱלֹהֵינוּ) שֶׁאָכַלְנוּ מִשֶּׁלּוֹ  *Company*
וּבְטוּבוֹ חָיִינוּ.

בָּרוּךְ (אֱלֹהֵינוּ) שֶׁאָכַלְנוּ מִשֶּׁלּוֹ  *Leader*
וּבְטוּבוֹ חָיִינוּ.
בָּרוּךְ הוּא וּבָרוּךְ שְׁמוֹ:


בָּרוּךְ אַתָּה יְיָ,
אֱלֹהֵינוּ מֶלֶךְ הָעוֹלָם,
הַזָּן אֶת הָעוֹלָם כֻּלּוֹ בְּטוּבוֹ;
בְּחֵן בְּחֶסֶד וּבְרַחֲמִים,
הוּא נוֹתֵן לֶחֶם לְכָל בָּשָׂר,
כִּי לְעוֹלָם חַסְדּוֹ.
וּבְטוּבוֹ הַגָּדוֹל
תָּמִיד לֹא חָסַר לָנוּ,
וְאַל יֶחְסַר לָנוּ
מָזוֹן לְעוֹלָם וָעֶד
בַּעֲבוּר שְׁמוֹ הַגָּדוֹל;
כִּי הוּא אֵל זָן וּמְפַרְנֵס לַכֹּל,
וּמֵטִיב לַכֹּל, וּמֵכִין מָזוֹן
לְכָל בְּרִיּוֹתָיו אֲשֶׁר בָּרָא.
בָּרוּךְ אַתָּה יְיָ,
הַזָּן אֶת הַכֹּל.

26

וּבְנֵה יְרוּשָׁלַיִם

עִיר הַקֹּדֶשׁ

בִּמְהֵרָה בְיָמֵינוּ.

בָּרוּךְ אַתָּה יְיָ,

בּוֹנֵה בְרַחֲמָיו יְרוּשָׁלָיִם.

אָמֵן.

עוֹשֶׂה שָׁלוֹם בִּמְרוֹמָיו,

הוּא יַעֲשֶׂה שָׁלוֹם

עָלֵינוּ וְעַל כָּל יִשְׂרָאֵל.

וְאִמְרוּ: אָמֵן.

יְיָ עֹז לְעַמּוֹ יִתֵּן;

יְיָ יְבָרֵךְ אֶת־עַמּוֹ בַשָּׁלוֹם.

*Music follows →*

27

## בִּרְכַּת הַמָּזוֹן – Grace after the Meal

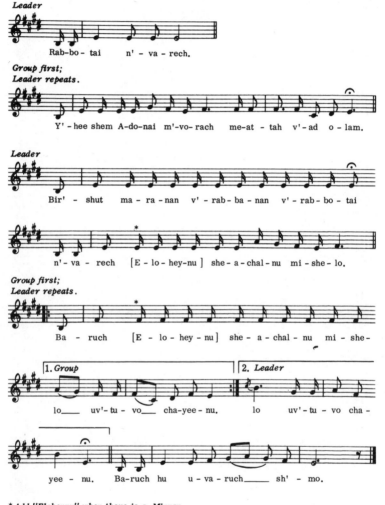

*Add "Eloheynu" when there is a Minyan.*

*Hazon et haolam:*

Ba - ruch at - tah— A - do - nai E - lo - hey - nu me-lech ha - o -

lam ha - zan et ha - o - lam kul - lo b'-tu - vo b' -

chen— b'che - sed uv' - ra - cha - meem hu no - ten

le - chem l'-chol ba - sar kee l' - o - lam— chas - do

uv' - tu - vo ha - ga - dol ta - meed lo cha - sar la - nu

v'al— yech-sar la-nu ma - zon l' - o - lam va - ed ba - a -

vur sh' - mo ha - ga - dol— kee hu El zan um'-far-nes la -

kol u - me - teev la - kol u - me-cheen ma - zon l' -

chol b'ree-yo-tav a - sher— ba - ra. Ba - ruch at - tah— A - do -

nai— ha - zan— et ha - kol.

**Leader:**

Uv'-neh Y'-ru-sha-la-yim eer ha - ko-desh bim'-he-rah b'- ya-

mey - nu.____ Ba - ruch at - tah A - do - nai____

**All:**

Bo - neh b'- ra-cha-mav Y'- ru-sha-la - yim, A - men.

**"Oseh Shalom"**

O - seh sha-lom bim'-ro-mav hu ya - a - seh sha - lom____ a-

ley - nu v'- al kol Yis-ra-el____ v'- im'-ru, A - men.

**"Adonai Oz"**

A - do-nai oz l'-am-mo yi - ten A - do - nai y'-vo-rech et am-

mo__ va-sha-lom. The Lord will give strength un-to His peo-ple, The

Lord will bless His peo-ple with peace. A - men.

30

# בִּרְכַּת הַמָּזוֹן בְּקִצְרָה — A Briefer Version

**Leader:**

Ba - ruch at-tah A-do - nai    E - lo - hey - nu me-lech ha - o - lam,
Be    praised Thou O Lord, our    God, King of the un - i - verse

**Company:**

Ha_____
who_____

zan    et____ ha - kol.
feed - est all man - kind.

O - seh sha - lom, shalom, sha-lom, bim' - ro - mav hu
O  He   who   mak - eth peace   in   His high plac - es

ya - a-seh sha-lom    a -    ley - nu,  o - seh sha-
may   He__ make peace for___ us! O He who mak-eth

lom,   sha - lom,   sha - lom   bim' - ro - mav   hu
peace_____    in    His    high   plac - es

ya - a-seh sha-lom   a - ley - nu v'-al___   kol  Yis - ra - el.
may__ He__ make peace for__ us__ and__   all   Is - ra - el.

**Leader:**                    **Company:**

V' - i - m'-ru        A -        men.
And let us say        A -        men.

31

## קִדּוּשׁ וּמוֹצִיא—Kiddush and Motzi for Shabbat Noon

וְשָׁמְרוּ בְנֵי־יִשְׂרָאֵל אֶת־הַשַּׁבָּת.
לַעֲשׂוֹת אֶת־הַשַּׁבָּת לְדֹרֹתָם
בְּרִית עוֹלָם.
בֵּינִי וּבֵין בְּנֵי יִשְׂרָאֵל
אוֹת הִוא לְעוֹלָם.
כִּי־שֵׁשֶׁת יָמִים עָשָׂה יְיָ
אֶת הַשָּׁמַיִם וְאֶת־הָאָרֶץ
וּבַיּוֹם הַשְּׁבִיעִי שָׁבַת וַיִּנָּפַשׁ:

The Israelite people shall keep the sabbath, observing the sabbath throughout the generations as a covenant for all time: it shall be a sign for all time between Me and the people of Israel. For in six days the Lord made heaven and earth, and on the seventh day He ceased from work and was refreshed.
*Exodus 31:16-17*

זָכוֹר אֶת־יוֹם הַשַּׁבָּת לְקַדְּשׁוֹ:
שֵׁשֶׁת יָמִים תַּעֲבֹד
וְעָשִׂיתָ כָּל־מְלַאכְתֶּךָ:
וְיוֹם הַשְּׁבִיעִי שַׁבָּת לַיהוָֹה אֱלֹהֶיךָ
לֹא־תַעֲשֶׂה כָל־מְלָאכָה
אַתָּה וּבִנְךָ וּבִתֶּךָ
עַבְדְּךָ וַאֲמָתְךָ וּבְהֶמְתֶּךָ
וְגֵרְךָ אֲשֶׁר בִּשְׁעָרֶיךָ:
כִּי שֵׁשֶׁת־יָמִים עָשָׂה יְיָ
אֶת־הַשָּׁמַיִם וְאֶת־הָאָרֶץ
אֶת־הַיָּם וְאֶת־כָּל־אֲשֶׁר־בָּם
וַיָּנַח בַּיּוֹם הַשְּׁבִיעִי
עַל־כֵּן בֵּרַךְ יְהוָֹה
אֶת־יוֹם הַשַּׁבָּת וַיְקַדְּשֵׁהוּ:

Remember the sabbath day and keep it holy. Six days you shall labor and do all your work, but the seventh day is a sabbath of the Lord your God: you shall not do any work—you, your son or daughter, your male or female slave, or your cattle, or the stranger who is within your settlements. For in six days the Lord made heaven and earth and sea, and all that is in them, and He rested on the seventh day; therefore the Lord blessed the sabbath day and hallowed it.
*Exodus 20:8-11*

Be praised, Lord our God,
Ruler of the Universe, Creator of the fruit of the vine.

בָּרוּךְ אַתָּה יְיָ,
אֱלֹהֵינוּ מֶלֶךְ הָעוֹלָם,
בּוֹרֵא פְּרִי הַגָּפֶן.

Be praised, Lord our God,
Ruler of the Universe, who
causes the earth to yield
food.

בָּרוּךְ אַתָּה יְיָ,
אֱלֹהֵינוּ מֶלֶךְ הָעוֹלָם,
הַמּוֹצִיא לֶחֶם מִן הָאָרֶץ:

*(Music above, pp. 18 and 20)*

מוֹצָאֵי שַׁבָּת
*Shabbat Night*

# הַבְדָּלָה — Prayers for the End of Shabbat

*To be said at the end of Shabbat, after it has gotten dark.*
*Prepare wine, a havdalah candle (or if unavailable, any other*
*candle), and a spice box containing a variety of spices (for*
*instance, cinnamon, cloves, allspice).*

**Leader:** Heavenly Father, in the twilight of this Shabbat, we turn our hearts unto Thee.

**Company:** Come ye, O house of Jacob, and let us walk in the light of the Lord.
Happy is the man who fears the Lord, who walks in His ways,
That raises up his heart to Him, in prayer and in thanksgiving .
The Lord is my deliverance, I trust and have no fear;
The Lord is my strength and my song, and He is become my salvation.
The Lord will give strength to His people, the Lord will bless His children with peace.
Peace, peace, unto him who is far off, and unto him who is near, saith the Lord.
I will lift up the cup of salvation,
I will call upon the name of the Lord:

*(Leader lifts the cup of wine, and all join in the blessing.)*

Be praised, Lord our God, Ruler of
the universe, who creates the fruit
of the vine.

בָּרוּךְ אַתָּה יְיָ,
אֱלֹהֵינוּ מֶלֶךְ הָעוֹלָם,
בּוֹרֵא פְּרִי הַגָּפֶן.

34

*(Leader drinks from the cup, lifts the spice box, and all say:)*

Lord of all worlds, Your Shabbat is coming to an end. Soon
we will turn to our work-day world. Keep within us, we
pray, the savor of this day of joy: the beauty of worship,
the delight of Your law, the warm fellowship of those who
gather in Your name. Let not our daily cares nor the un-
certainties of tomorrow take from us the added soul with
which Shabbat has blessed us. But let the fragrance of this
day abide within the sanctuary of our spirit.

| | |
|---|---|
| Be praised, Lord our God, Ruler of the Universe, who creates the varied kinds of spices. | בָּרוּךְ אַתָּה יְיָ, אֱלֹהֵינוּ מֶלֶךְ הָעוֹלָם, בּוֹרֵא מִינֵי בְשָׂמִים. |

*(Leader shakes the spices, smells them, and passes them on so
that all may enjoy their fragrance. He then gives the havdalah
candle to a young person, lights it, and says the blessing.)*

| | |
|---|---|
| Be praised, Lord our God, Ruler of the Universe who creates the lights and fires. | בָּרוּךְ אַתָּה יְיָ, אֱלֹהֵינוּ מֶלֶךְ הָעוֹלָם, בּוֹרֵא מְאוֹרֵי הָאֵשׁ. |

*(Leader lifts Kiddush cup again, and says the blessing.)*

בָּרוּךְ אַתָּה יְיָ,

אֱלֹהֵינוּ מֶלֶךְ הָעוֹלָם,

הַמַּבְדִּיל בֵּין קֹדֶשׁ לְחוֹל,

בֵּין אוֹר לְחֹשֶׁךְ,

בֵּין יִשְׂרָאֵל לָעַמִּים,

בֵּין יוֹם הַשְּׁבִיעִי

לְשֵׁשֶׁת יְמֵי הַמַּעֲשֶׂה.

בָּרוּךְ אַתָּה יְיָ,

הַמַּבְדִּיל בֵּין קֹדֶשׁ לְחוֹל.

*(The candle is extinguished in the wine.)*

### ALL TOGETHER:

Be praised Lord our God, Ruler of the Universe, who distinguishes between the sacred and the profane, between light and darkness, between the seventh day and the six days of labor. Help us, too, we pray, to distinguish between that which is real and enduring, and that which is fleeting and vain. May we value affection and helpfulness more than power and possession, that the joy of a good deed may be our greatest delight, and our zeal for justice outweigh all selfish pursuits.

Grant unto us a good week, a week of courage and faithfulness, a week of health and prosperity, a week of blessing and of peace. Amen.

# הַבְדָּלָה – Havdalah

# הַמַבְדִיל – Hamavdeel

**Quietly rhythmic**

Ha - mav - deel beyn ko - desh beyn ko - desh l'-

chol cha - to - tey - nu hu yim - chol___

___ Zar - ey - nu v'-chas - pe - nu yar - beh ka -

chol v' - cha - ko - cha - veem ba - lay - lah.___ *rit.*

**Chorus** *a tempo*

Sha - vu - a tov, sha - vu - a tov, sha - vu - a tov, sha - vu - a

tov, sha - vu - a tov, sha - vu - a tov, sha - vu - a tov, sha - vu - a tov.

He who distinguishes between holy day and every day, may He forgive our sins, and increase our people and its welfare like the sand and like the stars at night.

May it be a good week!

הַמַבְדִיל בֵּין קֹדֶשׁ לְחוֹל,

חַטֹּאתֵינוּ הוּא יִמְחוֹל,

זַרְעֵנוּ וְכַסְפֵּנוּ יַרְבֶּה כַּחוֹל

וְכַכּוֹכָבִים בַּלָּיְלָה.

שָׁבוּעַ טוֹב . . .

38

# אֵלִיָּהוּ – Eliyahu

*(Elijah the Prophet is now remembered, for he has traditionally symbolized our hope for the messianic age.)*

Eliyahu Hanavi, Eliyahu Ha-Tishbi,
Eliyahu, Eliyahu, Eliyahu Ha-Giladi.
Lord, Your Kingdom soon be here,
Speed the coming of Your cheer;
Make all strife and evil cease,
Speed the coming of Your peace.
Eliyahu Hanavi, Eliyahu Ha-Tishbi,
Eliyahu, Eliyahu, Eliyahu Ha-Giladi.

אֵלִיָּהוּ הַנָּבִיא,
אֵלִיָּהוּ הַתִּשְׁבִּי,
אֵלִיָּהוּ הַגִּלְעָדִי,
בִּמְהֵרָה בְיָמֵינוּ
יָבֹא אֵלֵינוּ,
עִם מָשִׁיחַ בֶּן דָּוִד.

# ZEMIROT
## Shabbat Songs

## נְקַדְּמָה פָנָיו — N'kadmah Fanav

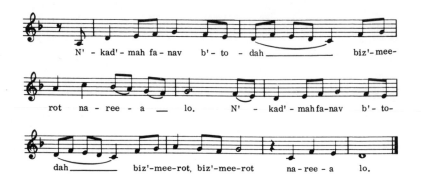

N' - kad' - mah fa - nav b' - to - dah _____ biz' - mee-
rot na - ree - a _ lo. N' - kad' - mahfa-nav b' - to-
dah _____ biz' - mee-rot, biz' - mee-rot na - ree - a lo.

We approach Him with thanks,
And sing before Him with joy.

*(Psalm 95:2)*

נְקַדְּמָה פָנָיו בְּתוֹדָה
בִּזְמִירוֹת נָרִיעַ לוֹ.

## Come, O Sabbath Day

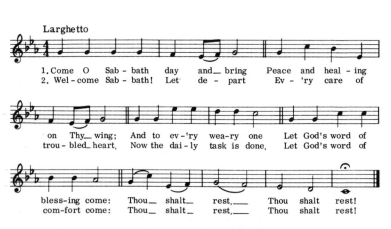

**Larghetto**

1. Come O Sab - bath day and_ bring Peace and heal - ing
2. Wel - come Sab - bath! Let de - part Ev - 'ry care of

on Thy_ wing; And to ev - 'ry wea - ry one Let God's word of
trou - bled_ heart, Now the dai - ly task is done, Let God's word of

bless - ing come: Thou_ shalt_ rest,___ Thou shalt rest!
com - fort come: Thou_ shalt_ rest,___ Thou shalt rest!

3. Work and sorrow cast away! With the setting of the sun,
Sabbath is for pray'r and play. Let God's cheering message come:
Thou shalt rest, Thou shalt rest!

42

## הַחַמָּה מֵרֹאש הָאִילָנוֹת—The Sun on the Tree Tops

**Slowly**

Ha - cham-mah me - rosh ha - ee - la - not nis - tal - kah. Bo -
The sun on the tree - tops no long - er is seen.___ Come

u ve - ney - tzey lik - rat Shab - bat ha - mal - kah. Hin - ney hee yo -
gath - er to wel-come the Sab - bath, our queen.___ Be - hold her de -

re - det, hak' - do - shah, ha - b'ru - chah. V' - im - mah mal -
scend - ing, the ho - ly, the blest,___ And with her the

a - chim tsva sha - lom um' - nu - chah, Bo - ee, bo - ee ha -
an - gels of peace and of rest.___ Draw near, O Queen, and

mal - kah! Bo - ee, bo - ee, ha - kal -
here___ a - bide; Draw near, draw near, O Sab - bath

lah! Sha - lom___ a - ley-chem, mal - a-chey ha - sha - lom.
bride. Peace al - so to you,___ ye an - gels of peace!

הַחַמָּה מֵרֹאש הָאִילָנוֹת נִסְתַּלְּקָה –

בֹּאוּ וְנֵצֵא לִקְרַאת שַׁבָּת הַמַּלְכָּה,

הִנֵּה הִיא יוֹרֶדֶת, הַקְּדוֹשָׁה, הַבְּרוּכָה,

וְעִמָּהּ מַלְאָכִים צְבָא שָׁלוֹם וּמְנוּחָה,

בֹּאִי בֹּאִי, הַמַּלְכָּה!

בֹּאִי בֹּאִי, הַמַּלְכָּה:

שָׁלוֹם עֲלֵיכֶם, מַלְאֲכֵי הַשָּׁלוֹם!

43

## שָׁלוֹם עֲלֵיכֶם – Shalom Aleychem

Peace unto you. Messengers of
the King of Kings,
The Holy One, praised be He.
May you come in peace, bless
in peace,
And go forth in peace.

שָׁלוֹם עֲלֵיכֶם מַלְאֲכֵי הַשָּׁרֵת,
מַלְאֲכֵי עֶלְיוֹן,
מִמֶּלֶךְ מַלְכֵי הַמְּלָכִים,
הַקָּדוֹשׁ בָּרוּךְ הוּא.

## לְכָה דוֹדִי – L'chah Dodee

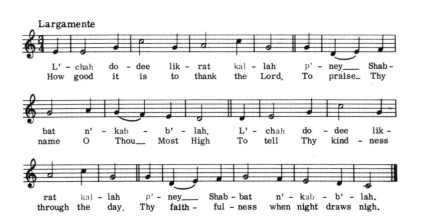

**Largamente**

L' - chah do - dee lik - rat kal - lah p' - ney___ Shab -
How good it is to thank the Lord, To praise_ Thy

bat n' - kab - b' - lah, L' - chah do - dee lik -
name O Thou__ Most High To tell Thy kind - ness

rat kal - lah p' - ney___ Shab - bat n' - kab - b' - lah.
through the day, Thy faith - ful - ness when night draws nigh.

Beloved come, the bride to meet,        לְכָה דוֹדִי לִקְרַאת כַּלָּה,
The princess Shabbat let us greet.      פְּנֵי שַׁבָּת נְקַבְּלָה.

*Another Version:*

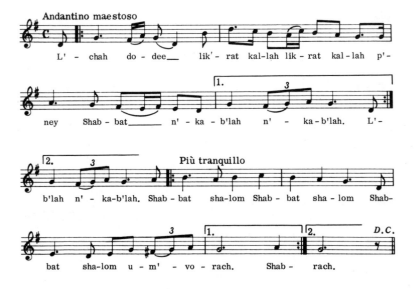

**Andantino maestoso**

L' - chah do - dee__ lik' - rat kal-lah lik - rat kal - lah p' -

ney Shab - bat_____ n' - ka - b'lah n' - ka-b'lah. L'-

**1.**

**2.**   **Più tranquillo**

b'lah n' - ka-b'lah. Shab - bat sha-lom Shab - bat sha - lom Shab-

**1.**  **2.**  **D.C.**

bat sha-lom u - m' - vo - rach. Shab - rach.

## הִנְנִי מוּכָן – Hin'nee Muchan Um'ezumman

**Slow but rhythmic**

Hin - n' - nee mu - chan u - m'zum - man

Hin - n' -nee mu-chan u - m'zum- man    Hin - n' - ni mu - chan u -

m'zum - man    Hin - n' - nee mu - chan u - m'zum - man.    *Fine*

K'mo    she - ka - tuv    ba - To    -    rah_____

1.
Hin - n' - nee mu - chan u - m'zum - man.

2.    *D.C. al Fine*
m'zum - man.

Lo, I am ready and prepared
To do what is written in the
Torah.

הִנְנִי מוּכָן וּמְזֻמָּן,
כְּמוֹ שֶׁכָּתוּב בַּתּוֹרָה.

46

# הֲשִׁיבֵנוּ – Hasheevenu

Turn us toward You, and we
   will return,
Renew our days as of old.

הֲשִׁיבֵנוּ אֵלֶיךָ וְנָשׁוּבָה,
חַדֵּשׁ יָמֵינוּ כְּקֶדֶם.

# יוֹם זֶה—Yom Zeh

This day is honored above all days,
For the Rock of the World rested on it.
Six days you shall do your work,
But the seventh day belongs to your God.
It is Shabbat, do no work on it,
For God himself did His labor in six days.

יוֹם זֶה מְכֻבָּד מִכָּל יָמִים.

כִּי בוֹ שָׁבַת צוּר עוֹלָמִים:

שֵׁשֶׁת יָמִים תַּעֲשֶׂה מְלַאכְתֶּךָ,

וְיוֹם הַשְּׁבִיעִי לֵאלֹהֶיךָ.

שַׁבָּת לֹא תַעֲשֶׂה בוֹ מְלָאכָה,

כִּי כֹל עָשָׂה שֵׁשֶׁת יָמִים.

48

# הַלְלוּהוּ — Hal'luhu

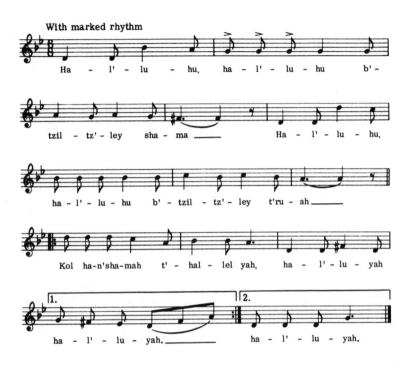

**With marked rhythm**

Ha - l' - lu - hu, ha - l' - lu - hu b' -
tzil - tz' - ley sha - ma ____ Ha - l' - lu - hu,
ha - l' - lu - hu b' - tzil - tz' - ley t'ru - ah ____
Kol ha-n'sha-mah t' - hal - lel yah, ha - l' - lu - yah

**1.** ha - l' - lu - yah. ____ **2.** ha - l' - lu - yah.

Praise Him with cymbals
  loud and noisy,
Let everything that has breath
Praise the Lord. Hallelujah.

*(Psalm 150:5, 6)*

הַלְלוּהוּ בְּצִלְצְלֵי־שָׁמַע,
הַלְלוּהוּ בְּצִלְצְלֵי תְרוּעָה,
כֹּל הַנְּשָׁמָה תְּהַלֵּל יָה הַלְלוּיָה.

49

## יָה רִבּוֹן — Yah Ribon

God of the World, eternity's sole Lord!
King over kings, be now Your Name adored!
Blessed are we to whom accord You do
This gladsome time Your wondrous ways to scan!
Early and late to You our praises ring,
Giver of life to every living thing!
Beasts of the field, and birds that heavenward wing,
Angelic hosts and all the sons of man!

יָהּ רִבּוֹן עָלַם וְעָלְמַיָּא,
אַנְתְּ הוּא מַלְכָּא מֶלֶךְ מַלְכַיָּא.
עוֹבַד גְּבוּרְתֵּךְ וְתִמְהַיָּא.
שַׁפִּיר קֳדָמָךְ לְהַחֲוָיֵהּ:
שְׁבָחִין אֲסַדֵּר צַפְרָא וְרַמְשָׁא,
לָךְ אֱלָהָא דִּי בְרָא כָל־נַפְשָׁא
עִירִין קַדִּישִׁין וּבְנֵי אֱנָשָׁא,
חֵיוַת בָּרָא וְעוֹפֵי שְׁמַיָּא:

50

## יִשְׂמְחוּ הַשָּׁמַיִם — Yism'chu Hashamayim

Let the heavens be glad and
    the earth rejoice,
Let the sea roar and the
    fullness thereof.

*(Psalm 96:11)*

יִשְׂמְחוּ הַשָּׁמַיִם
וְתָגֵל הָאָרֶץ
יִרְעַם הַיָּם וּמְלֹאוֹ.

51

## הַיּוֹם יוֹם שַׁבָּת—Hayom Yom Shabbat

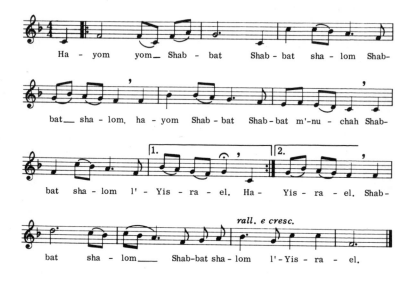

Ha - yom yom_ Shab - bat Shab - bat sha - lom Shab-
bat_ sha - lom, ha - yom Shab - bat Shab - bat m'-nu - chah Shabbat sha - lom l' - Yis - ra - el. Ha- Yis - ra - el. Shabbat sha - lom_ Shab-bat sha - lom l' - Yis - ra - el.

Today is Shabbat,
A Shabbat of peace and rest
   for Israel.

הַיּוֹם יוֹם שַׁבָּת,
שַׁבָּת שָׁלוֹם.
הַיּוֹם שַׁבָּת,
שַׁבָּת מְנוּחָה,
שַׁבָּת שָׁלוֹם לְיִשְׂרָאֵל.

# וְהָאֵר עֵינֵינוּ — V'haer Eyneynu

Bouncy (♩=126)

(Clap Hands)

V'- ha - er ey-ney-nu b'- to - ra - te-cha v' - dab - bek li - bey - nu b'-

mitz - vo - te - cha. V' - ya ched l' - va - ve-nu l'-

a - ha - vah ul'-yir-ah et sh' - me - cha. V'- et sh' - me - cha. V'-

lo_____ ne - vosh v' - lo_____ ni - ka -

lem. V' - lo_____ ni - ka - lem_____

l' - o - lam va - ed. V' - ed. V'-

ha - er ey-ney-nu b'- to - ra - te-cha v' - dab - bek li - bey - nu b'-

53

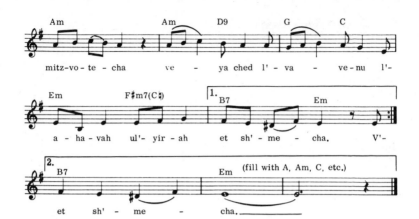

Brighten our vision
Through Your Torah,
And attach our hearts
To Your mitzvot.
May we love and revere
    Your name,
So that we may be sustained
    forever.

וְהָאֵר עֵינֵינוּ בְּתוֹרָתֶךָ,
וְדַבֵּק לִבֵּנוּ בְּמִצְוֹתֶיךָ.
וְיַחֵד לְבָבֵנוּ לְאַהֲבָה
וּלְיִרְאָה אֶת־שְׁמֶךָ,
וְלֹא נֵבוֹשׁ לְעוֹלָם וָעֶד.

# יִשְׂמְחוּ בְמַלְכוּתְךָ—Yism'chu V'malchut'cha

They who keep the Shabbat and call it a delight shall rejoice in Your Kingdom;

The people who hallow the seventh day, all of them shall be filled and delighted with Your goodness.

For You found pleasure in the seventh day and hallowed it, calling it "the joy of days," in remembrance of the work of Creation.

יִשְׂמְחוּ בְמַלְכוּתְךָ
שׁוֹמְרֵי שַׁבָּת וְקוֹרְאֵי עֹנֶג.
עַם מְקַדְּשֵׁי שְׁבִיעִי
כֻּלָּם יִשְׂבְּעוּ וְיִתְעַנְּגוּ מִטּוּבֶךָ.
וּבַשְּׁבִיעִי רָצִיתָ בּוֹ
וְקִדַּשְׁתּוֹ,
חֶמְדַּת יָמִים אוֹתוֹ קָרֵאתָ,
זֵכֶר לְמַעֲשֵׂה בְרֵאשִׁית.

# אֵלִי אֵלִי — Elee Elee

E - lee  E - lee  she - lo  yig-ga  mer  l'- o - lam  ha-
chol  v'- ha - yam  rish - rush  shel  ha - ma - yim  b'-
rak  ha - sha - ma - yim  t'fil - lat  ha - a - dam  ha-
chol  v'- ha - yam  rish - rush  shel  ha - ma - yim  b'-
rak  ha - sha - ma - yim  t'fil - lat  ha - a - dam.

My God, my God, may these
    never cease:
The sand and the sea, the
    roar of the waters,
The lightning of heaven, the
    prayer of man.

אֵלִי אֵלִי,
שֶׁלֹּא יִגָּמֵר לְעוֹלָם:
הַחוֹל וְהַיָּם,
רִשְׁרוּשׁ שֶׁל הַמַּיִם,
בְּרַק הַשָּׁמַיִם,
תְּפִלַּת הָאָדָם.

## עוֹשֶׂה שָׁלוֹם—Oseh Shalom

ya - a - seh sha - lom        sha - lom a - ley - nu v'-

al kol Yis - ra - el.                                    O -

al kol Yis - ra - el.

He who makes peace on high,
May He make peace for us.
And for all Israel,
And say ye: "Amen."

עוֹשֶׂה שָׁלוֹם בִּמְרוֹמָיו
הוּא יַעֲשֶׂה שָׁלוֹם עָלֵינוּ
וְעַל כָּל יִשְׂרָאֵל,
וְאִמְרוּ : אָמֵן.

# SHABBAT
## IN
## TORAH AND TRADITION

## The Biblical Basis

In its historical importance and as an instrument for preserving Judaism, Shabbat is the most importanct of all Jewish institutions. It is *the* holy day. Coming with weekly regularity, it constantly keeps alive the spirit of holiness without which Judaism could not be sustained.

The Torah designates eight days in the calendar as holy convocations—Shabbat, first day of Pesach, seventh day of Pesach, Shavuot, Rosh Hashanah, Yom Kippur, first day of Succot, and eighth day of Succot. All are "sabbaths" in their own right, whether falling on the seventh day of the week or on another day. The term "shabbat" means "rest" or "refraining from work." Concerning all eight holy convocations, the Scripture says: "You shall do no manner of work."

In theory, all eight holy days have equal weight and importance, yet it is clear that the Torah puts greater emphasis on the weekly Shabbat than on any of the other days. It alone is included in the Decalogue. Equally striking is the fact that in the opening verses of the Torah Shabbat is made the culmination of the whole of God's work of creation. No other holy day is mentioned in the creation story.

### Observance

The most important biblical passages (a selection of which appears in "Selected Readings") state Shabbat was instituted by God because, after creating the world in six days, He Himself rested on the seventh day and blessed and hallowed that day, setting it apart from the rest of the week. Shabbat, thus, is a memorial of the six days of creation.

Shabbat serves as a reminder of the time when the Israelites were slaves in Egypt and were redeemed from their bondage by God. Shabbat is the sign of a perpetual covenant between God and Israel—that Israel may acknowledge God and know that it is He who sanctifies the people.

Every member of an Israelite household must rest on the seventh day. This includes the master as well as the man-servant and maid-servant, children, and even strangers who reside within an Israelite community. Work animals are also to be relieved of work on this day.

The following forms of labor are specifically prohibited: gathering food, gathering wood, plowing, harvesting, baking and cooking food, carrying burdens into the city or in or out of a house, selling grain and corn or other victuals, carrying on business in any form, treading winepresses, loading animals with corn, wine, figs, grapes and other burdens, bringing fish or any kind of ware into the city. One may not leave his "place" on Shabbat, meaning that one may not go beyond the limits of his city or village. It is forbidden to kindle a fire on Shabbat. The Sabbath is to be kept "holy," meaning that it is to be distinguished and set apart from the rest of the week. Profanation of the Shabbat by Israel aroused the wrath of God, resulting in the destruction of Jerusalem and the dispersion of the people. By honoring the day of Shabbat, Israel will find safety and security.

Sacrificial offerings constituted the main form of Shabbat worship in the Bible. Psalm 92, however, declares that it is good to give thanks to the Lord and to sing praises to His name "with an instrument of ten strings and with the psaltery; with a solemn sound upon the harp." Joyous music thus accompanied the sacrificial Temple worship on Shabbat in biblical times. Further, Isaiah's reference to Shabbat as "a delight" had far-reaching implications in later generations, as it suggested that the day be celebrated in the spirit of joy and gladness.

Finally, Shabbat represents an intimation of mankind's future. The time will come when "from one new moon to another and from one sabbath to another" all men will come to worship God.

Since biblical law was only in a few instances explicit in stating what was meant by Shabbat rest or in defining what constituted work, it remained for the rabbinical authorities in Mishnah and Talmud and codes to be more specific when applying the Sabbath law to the countless facets of life encountered by a Jew on the seventh day.

Most of talmudic law relating to Shabbat is an extension or embellishment of biblical rules, taking into account every possibility that might arise either in fulfillment of the law or its violation. By deduction and inference, a great mass of halachic (legal) material came into being. Both the broad, general principles of Shabbat observance and the minutiae were incorporated into the halachah. To the rabbis of the tal- mudic age, the Torah was the revealed word of God given to a people consecrated to the task of living according to its statutes and teachings. God had graciously granted to man reason and understanding, enabling him to deduce through logical principles the specific application of the law in every- day life from the broader biblical principles. To the rabbis, what was written in the Torah and what could be inferred from the written word represented the divine will. A Jew had no alternative but to regulate his life in accordance with both. In contrast to the written law of the Bible, the new material arrived at through inference and deduction was called "oral law," though it too was eventually written down in the sixty- three books comprising the Mishnah and Talmud tractates and in a number of Midrashic works as well.

The Mishnah, the core of the talmudic literature (codified about 200 C.E.), lists thirty-nine major categories of work prohibited on Shabbat, a few taken directly from the Torah itself and most arrived at through inference. These are:
Sowing, ploughing, reaping, binding sheaves, threshing, win- nowing, cleansing crops, grinding, sifting, kneading, baking, shearing wool, washing or beating or dyeing it, spinning, weaving, making two loops, weaving two threads, separating

two threads, tying a knot, loosening a knot, sewing two stitches, tearing in order to sew two stitches, hunting a gazelle, slaughtering or flaying or salting it or curing its skin, scraping it or cutting it up, writing two letters of the alphabet, erasing in order to write two letters, building, pulling down, extinguishing a fire, lighting a fire, striking with a hammer and carrying an object from one domain to another. (Shabbat 7:2)

In addition to the above, numerous minor categories of work and activity prohibited on Shabbat were deduced from the major categories. These minor prohibitions were instituted as "fences" to ward off the possibility of committing a major violation. Thus, one may not ride an animal on the Sabbath lest he be tempted to break a branch off a tree for use in guiding the animal. The prohibition against riding an animal becomes a preventative to the more serious offence of breaking a branch off a tree. Similarly, one may not blow the shofar in the synagogue on Rosh Hashanah if that day falls on Shabbat, not because Scripture forbids blowing the shofar on Shabbat (which it does not), but because one may forget to bring the instrument to the synagogue prior to Shabbat, and by bringing it on that day violate the more stringent prohibition against carrying an object on Shabbat from one domain to another or the distance of four cubits in the public domain.

Lenient Interpretation

While much of the Shabbat law in the Talmud appears as a heaping of prohibition upon prohibition, in actuality a large part of the halachah is an attempt by the rabbis to lessen the harshness and severity of the biblical law by means of a more liberal interpretation. Biblical law had stated: "You shall kindle no fire in all your habitations on the day of Shabbat." (Exodus 35:3) This could be interpreted to mean that no light or heat in any form would be permitted in a home from the beginning to the end of Shabbat. The rabbinical authorities permitted light and heat on Shabbat if the fire had been kindled before Shabbat began.

The Christian Gospels accused Judaism of forbidding healing of the sick on Shabbat. Actually, rabbinic law put all Shabbat restrictions aside when life and health were at stake. Maimonides sums up the Talmudic position in the following words:

The Shabbat commandment, like all other commandments, may be set aside if human life is in danger. Accordingly, if a person is dangerously ill, whatever a skilled local physician considers necessary may be done for him on Shabbat. . . .

As long as treatment is necessary and danger—or possibility of danger—persists, even a hundred days of Shabbat may be violated. One may light a lamp, extinguish a lamp that is disturbing the patient, slaughter an animal, bake, cook, or heat water for the patient to drink or wash with. In general, insofar as the needs of a person who is dangerously ill are concerned, the Shabbat is the same as a weekday.(Maimonides, *Yad,* Hilchot Shabbat II:1-3).

Biblical law had made it mandatory that a new-born child be circumcised on the eighth day after his birth and the question arose concerning the propriety of circumcision on Shabbat. Since doing work profaned the Shabbat, and since Scripture states, "He who profanes it will surely die" (Exodus 31:14), one might seek to avoid performing a circumcision on that day on the ground that it is like manual labor. The rabbis, however, permitted circumcision on Shabbat if that was the eighth day, but if for reasons of health the circumcision had to be postponed it could not then be held on Shabbat.

Scripture had stated, "Let no man leave his place on the seventh day." (Exodus 16:29) In this context, "place" was taken to mean the limits of the city. Since the Torah fails to define the dimensions of this limit, the rabbis assumed that it could be the size of the Israelite camp in the wilderness, which was twelve miles. In addition, the rabbis permitted one to walk a distance of two thousand cubits (a cubit measures about eighteen inches) in any direction outside the city limits.

## A Day of Delight

While extending and enlarging upon the prohibitions of the day, or finding ways to be lenient in observing the biblical law, occupy much of talmudic discussion concerning Shabbat, the rabbis also gave considerable thought to making the seventh day a day of beauty, joy, and spiritual enhancement. Scripture had commanded: "Remember the Shabbat day to keep it holy" (Exodus 20:8), and "Observe the Shabbat day to keep it holy" (Deuteronomy 5:12), and also, "You shall call Shabbat a delight and the holy of the Lord honorable." (Isaiah 58:13) The key words in these verses are "remember," "observe," "holy," "delight," and "honor."

One remembers and observes the day to keep it holy, the rabbis said, by reciting words of praise and santification both at the beginning of the day and at its termination. Hence, the Kiddush, a benediction for sanctification of the day, is recited when Shabbat commences, and the Havdalah, a benediction which declares the distinction between the holy and profane, is recited when the holy day has come to an end. The rabbis ruled that the Kiddush be recited over a cup of wine, but permitted bread to be used for the Kiddush if wine was lacking. (For Havdalah, any drink except water was allowed, but alcoholic beverages were preferred.) Originally the Kiddush was established as a home ceremony to be carried out only where the Shabbat eve meal was eaten. Later it was added to the Shabbat eve service in the synagogue for the benefit of wayfarers who ate their meals there. In the Havdalah ceremony, benedictions were also recited over spices and over a light which was kindled. In answer to the question, "Why the benediction over spices?" the rabbis answered, "Because one's soul is saddened by the outgoing of Shabbat, and therefore one should soothe and cheer it by means of fragrant odors."

In honoring the day and making it a delight, it became a religious duty before Shabbat commenced to put one's home or room in order, wash hands, face, and feet in hot water, and put on clean clothes which had not been worn on weekdays. One should receive the Shabbat, the rabbis taught, as if one were going forth to meet the king. It was the practice of the sages of old, we are told, to gather together their disciples on Friday night, put on their best clothes, and say, "Come, let us go forth to meet Sabbath, the king." ( Hilchot Shabbat 30:2)*

Delight in the Shabbat also meant preparing meals consisting of the richest foods and choicest beverages one could afford. Those who lived in luxury and wealth and had rich foods and beverages as their daily fare were required to make their Shabbat meals different in some way from those of weekdays. It was a religious duty to eat three meals on Shabbat, one in the evening and the others in the morning and the afternoon, in contrast to the usual custom of eating two meals on weekdays. Even the poor and those who lived on charity were required to eat the three meals.

Public fasting on Shabbat was prohibited. If a public fast day coincided with Shabbat, the fast was moved over to the following day, or, for the fast of Esther, to the previous Thursday. (An exception to this rule was made when the Day of Atonement fell on Shabbat.) Fasting was forbidden on Shabbat even when a community was in distress and beset with great troubles, and it was also not permitted in such circumstances to cry out to God on the seventh day in supplication for grace and mercy. Hence the twelve middle benedictions of the Amidah recited on weekdays, which are prayers of supplication, were removed from the Shabbat Amidah and replaced by a single benediction which blessed God for hallowing the Shabbat. While it was customary for a community in times of tribulation to sound the shofar on weekdays, as a cry of distress or an act of supplication, this was not allowed on Shabbat, except in instances where the city was under siege or endangered by flood waters or a ship was

*In another tradition, Shabbat is called a queen.

66

being storm-tossed at sea. In such circumstances, the shofar could be sounded on Shabbat to summon help.

## A Day Set Apart

The whole point underlying talmudic interpretation of Shabbat law was to distinguish the seventh day from the rest of the week, for this was the basic meaning of the biblical command "to make it holy." A holy day is a day set apart, a day that is unique.

In both Bible and Talmud, emphasis was put on the concept of Shabbat as the sign of an eternal covenant between God and Israel. Observance of Shabbat became the instrument for a great weekly affirmation by Israel of that covenant. Thus, as Israel hallowed the seventh day, a day consecrated to God, thereby affirming the covenant, so did it become a people consecrated to God, a holy people.

Christianity has been highly critical of Shabbat rules developed by the rabbinic tradition, claiming that they are casuistic, burdensome, and foolish. The stories in the New Testament of the plucking of ears of corn on Shabbat by the disciples and of the healing by Jesus of the man with the withered hand (Mark 2:23-3:6) would imply that Christianity offered a way of observing the day far superior to that offered by Pharisaic Judaism. (Christian strictures with respect to the Jewish Shabbat must be seen in the light of its acceptance of the pagan Sunday as its day for religious emphasis.)

Contrary to the Christian opinion, Shabbat was far from being a burden to the devout Jew. The minutiae of law as well as its broad principles gave him total release from toil in every possible form. The fact that he was not permitted even to discuss business matters or matters related to his livelihood freed his mind completely from the cares and anxieties of the week. Every seventh day, therefore, was refreshment of both body and spirit, and he was truly a free man.

# SELECTED READINGS

# FROM THE BIBLE

The heaven and the earth were finished, and all their array. And on the seventh day God finished the work which He had been doing, and He ceased on the seventh day from all the work which He had done. And God blessed the seventh day and declared it holy, because on it God ceased from all the work of creation which He had done.

*(Genesis 2:1-3)*

Remember the sabbath day and keep it holy. Six days you shall labor and do all your work, but the seventh day is a sabbath of the Lord your God: you shall not do any work, you, your son or daughter, your male or female slave, or your cattle, or the stranger who is within your settlements. For in six days the Lord made heaven and earth and sea, and all that is in them, and He rested on the seventh day; therefore the Lord blessed the sabbath day and hallowed it.

*(Exodus 20:8-11)*

Observe the sabbath day and keep it holy, as the Lord your God has commanded you. Six days you shall labor and do all your work but the seventh day is a sabbath of the Lord your God: you shall not do any work, you, your son or your daughter, your male or female slave, your ox or your ass, or any of your cattle, or the stranger in your settlements, so that your male and female slave may rest as you do. Remember that you were a slave in the land of Egypt and the Lord your God freed you from there with a mighty hand and an outstretched arm; therefore the Lord your God has commanded you to observe the sabbath day.

*(Deuteronomy 5:12-15)*

Thus says the Lord: Take heed for the sake of your souls, and carry no burden on the sabbath day, nor bring it in by the gates of Jerusalem.

*(Jeremiah 17:21)*

So I caused them to go forth out of the land of Egypt, and brought them into the wilderness. And I gave them My statutes, and taught them My ordinances, which if a man do, he shall live by them. Moreover also I gave them My sabbaths, to be a sign between Me and them, that they might know that I am the Lord that sanctifies them.

But the house of Israel rebelled against Me in the wilderness; they walked not in My statutes, and they rejected My ordinances, which if a man do, he shall live by them, and My sabbaths they greatly profaned; then I said I would pour out My fury upon them in the wilderness, to consume them.

*(Ezekiel 20:10-13)*

If you turn away your foot because of the sabbath,
From pursuing your business on My holy day;
And call the sabbath a delight
And the holy of the Lord honorable;
And if you will honor it without doing what you always do,
Not pursuing your business, nor even speaking of it;
Then shall you delight yourself in the Lord,
And I will make you to ride upon the high places of the earth,
And I will nourish you with the heritage of Jacob your father;
For the mouth of the Lord has spoken it.

*(Isaiah 58:13-14)*

## FROM TALMUD AND MIDRASH

Rabbi Jochanan said in the name of Rabbi Shimon ben Yochai: All mitzvot which the Holy One, praised be He, gave to Israel, He gave in public, except the mitzvah of Shabbat which He gave in private, as it said: "It is a sign between Me and the children of Israel forever." (Exodus 31:17) (*Talmud*)

The expression that Shabbat is "a sign forever" informs you that Shabbat will never cease from Israel. (*Midrash*)

71

Said the Holy One, praised be He, to Israel:

If you will manage to observe Shabbat I will reckon it to you as if you had observed all the mitzvot in the Torah; and if you desecrate Shabbat I will reckon it to you as if you had desecrated all the mitzvot. (*Midrash*)

There are three things that testify for each other: Israel, Shabbat, and the Holy One, praised be He. Israel and the Holy One testify that Shabbat is a day of rest; Israel and Shabbat testify that the Holy One, praised be He, is unique in this world. The Holy One and Shabbat testify for Israel. (*Midrash*)

Rabbi Berachya said in the name of Rabbi Chiyya bar Abba: Shabbat was given only for pleasure. Rabbi Chaggai said in the name of Rabbi Shemuel bar Nachman: Shabbat was given only for the study of Torah. Actually there is no contradiction between these two statements. The one which says Shabbat was given for pleasure applies to the scholars, for they labor in Torah all week long and on Shabbat they should have pleasure; while those that say that Shabbat is for the study of Torah applies to those who all week are busy in other labor, but comes Shabbat they should occupy themselves with Torah. (*Midrash*)

One Shabbat in this world is worth sixty in the world to come.

(*Midrash*)

## FROM MEDIEVAL SOURCES

A Jew is obligated to eat three meals on Shabbat: one on Erev Shabbat, one in the morning, and one in the afternoon. This applies even to the poor who live from charity.

One must not fast nor sorrow on Shabbat.

(*Maimonides*)

Shabbat outweighs all the mitzvot in the Torah. Hence he who desecrates Shabbat in public is like one who serves idols.

A Jew who greets his neighbour on Shabbat does not say to him as he would on a weekday: "Good morning" or "Good

72

day"; he must say to him: "Shabbat Shalom" or "Shabbat Tov," in order to observe the biblical injunction: "Remember Shabbat to keep it holy."

*(Isaiah Halevi Hurwitz)*

A God-fearing Jew will not sit down for his Shabbat eve meal until he has given or sent something from his table to the poor. It is even better to invite a young man or orphan or guest to his Shabbat table.

*(Jospe Hahn)*

These customs were observed amongst the pious Jews of Safed: They bathed on Erev Shabbat, they put on white clothes, and at the three meals they sang many songs of praise to God.

*(Abraham Halevi)*

## FROM MODERN LITERATURE

### The Whole People

The basic principle in the observance of the commandments of our Sages is the fact that the whole nation has accepted them, so that the honor of the nation, its historical influence, and its eternal, divine quality are incarnate in them.

*(Abraham Isaac Kuk)*

### No Puritan Observance

The Jewish Sabbath is not a Puritan Sabbath; it is not a gloomy or a sad day. It is rather a day of joy and of pleasure. All the restrictions imposed upon us during this day, as *e.g.,* to refrain from work and travel, are intended primarily not to impose burdens upon us, but rather to give us full leisure and thus to increase our joys and our pleasure on this sacred day. Our spiritual as well as our material life is to be made richer, more pleasant and more delightful by our leisure on the Sabbath day and by the observance of its ceremonies. It is a religious duty to have pleasure and delight, Oneg Shabbat, on this day.

*(Jacob Z. Lauterbach)*

## Reward and Punishment

If we declare that the observance of the Sabbath brings deep and abiding rewards to the Jew, that it recreates his spirit as it regenerates his physical and nervous system, that it brings him into communion with God, links him with the profoundest aspirations of Israel, and draws him into the orbit of Torah, then it follows inescapably that failure to observe the Sabbath brings its penalty in the impoverishment of the spirit, in the denudation of Jewish values, and in the alienation of the violators from the Jewish community, literally, "that soul is cut off from its kinsmen."

*(Robert Gordis)*

## Liberation from the Demonic

The seventh day, which had even previously been regarded as "holy," that is, as something excepted from the general series of days, and which accordingly enjoyed taboos peculiar to itself, was now to belong entirely to YHVH. It was to be "holy unto YHVH." Just as on the Passover the shepherds brought the first-born of every flock to the God, so should they now bring a tribute of their time: the seventh day. Henceforward it was no longer "holy" in itself, no longer something uncanny, charged with magic, a day for dread and caution, to be treated with all kinds of negative and positive rites. It was hallowed by the very fact that it was hallowed unto YHVH: it was hallowed through him and through the contact with him. This God had indeed absorbed everything demonic in himself, but whoever established communion with him was liberated from all demoniality; and the seventh days hallowed unto him were times of joy.

*(Martin Buber)*

## Body and Spirit

The affirmation of earthly needs and vital impulses is characteristic of the whole system of the law of Judaism. Sabbath and holidays are not observed "spiritually," nor should they be so observed. Man is not a spirit. On the Sabbath, therefore, not only the soul should find peace, but the body too should rest. One celebrates the day not only by meditation and prayer, but also by wearing Sabbath clothes and by partaking of the Sabbath meals. The Sabbath meal itself is a mitzvah; it is divine service. And if properly performed, it is a service of a far higher quality than that of prayer and meditation alone; it is the service of the whole man.

The enjoyment of the Sabbath is neither spiritual nor material; it is *wholly* human. Body and spirit celebrate the Sabbath in communion. The Jew who keeps the Sabbath may say that the material enjoyments of the day enhance his spiritual elation and that his spiritual elation renders the material enjoyments more gratifying. In the unifying act of the mitzvah the Sabbath acts as "a spice" to the palate and as an exhilarating joy for the spirit of man.

*(Eliezer Berkovits)*

## Shabbat as Poetry

Ceremonies represent the poetry and the drama of religion translated in forms that are universally understandable. They speak to the emotions, and invest life with holiness. In the view of tradition, they are to be kept not because of their attractiveness, but rather because they were commanded by God. *Mitzvot lo lehanot nitnu*—"the commandments were not given for the purpose of affording pleasure."

*(Samuel S. Cohon)*

## Holiness in Time

The Bible is more concerned with time than with space. It sees the world in the dimension of time. It pays more attention to generations, to events, than to countries, to things; it is more concerned with history than with geography. To understand the teaching of the Bible, one must accept its premise that time has a meaning which is at least equal to that of space; that time has a significance and sovereignty of its own.

75

One of the most distinguished words in the Bible is the word *kadosh,* holy; a word which more than any other is representative of the mystery and majesty of the divine. Now what was the first holy object in the history of the world? Was it a mountain? Was it an altar?

It is, indeed, a unique occasion at which the distinguished word *kadosh* is used for the first time: in the book of Genesis at the end of the story of creation. How extremely significant is the fact that it is applied to time: "And God blessed the seventh *day* and made it holy" (Genesis 2:3). There is no reference in the record of creation to any object in space that would be endowed with the quality of holiness.

This is a radical departure from accustomed religious thinking. The mythical mind would expect that, after heaven and earth have been established, God would create a holy place—a holy mountain or a holy spring—whereupon a sanctuary is to be established. Yet it seems as if to the Bible it is *holiness in time,* the Sabbath, which comes first.

The meaning of the Sabbath is to celebrate time rather than space. Six days a week we live under the tyranny of things of space; on the Sabbath we try to become attuned to *holiness in time.* It is a day on which we are called upon to share in what is eternal in time, to turn from the results of creation to the mystery of creation; from the world of creation to the creation of the world.

*(Abraham J. Heschel)*

## Unique Moment

In the light of *doing,* of the right doing in which we experience the reality of the Law, explanations are of superficial and subsidiary importance. And, in the doing, there is even less room for the converse wisdom (which in hours of weakness and emptiness we gladly clutch at for comfort), that historical and sociological explanations may be true, and that Law is important because it alone guarantees the unity of the people in space and through time. Such timid insight lies behind and beneath the moment of doing, in which we experience just this moment; it is this experience of the theo-human reality of the commandment that permits us to pray: "Blessed art Thou. . . ."

In this immediacy we may not "express" God (*Gott aussprechen*), but rather "address" God (*Gott ansprechen*), in the individual commandment. For whoever seeks to express him will discover that he who cannot be expressed, will become he who cannot be found. Only in the commandment can the voice of him who commands be heard. No matter how well the written word may fit in with our own thoughts, it cannot give us the faith that creation is completed, to the degree that we experience this by keeping the Sabbath, and inaugurating it with, "And the heaven and the earth were completed." Not that doing necessarily results in hearing and understanding. But one hears differently when one hears in the doing.

All the days of the year Balaam's talking ass may be a mere fairy tale, but not on the Sabbath wherein this portion is read in the synagogue, when it speaks to me out of the open Torah. But if not a fairy tale, what then? I cannot say right now; if I should think about it today, when it is past, and try to say what it is, I should probably only utter the platitude that it is a fairy tale. But on that day, in that very hour, it is—well, certainly not a fairy tale, but that which is communicated to me provided I am able to fulfill the command of the hour, namely, to open my ears.

*(Franz Rosenzweig)*


Between Kiddush and Havdalah

Whatever the case with the Sabbath in other religions, there is not the least suggestion of "blueness" about it in its original, Jewish incarnation. On the contrary, it is very much a day of joy and lightness of heart. In the synagogue it is marked

77

by hymns and elaborated worship; in the home by the donning of one's best and gayest clothes, by the kindling of candles at its inception in the sunset hours, by the Kiddush, an inaugural prayer of benediction intoned over a wine cup, by festive meals and table songs, by relaxation, conversation, and informal study, and at its very conclusion by the Havdalah, a picturesque ceremonial of division wherein the gladsome and sacred day is sent away with the savor of wine, the fragrance of sweet spices, and the light of a candle.

Beautiful in itself, the beauty of the Jewish Sabbath has been enhanced by a rich embroidery of folklore; its envisagement, for example, as a fair and chaste bride descending on the rays of the setting sun to her faithful one; the legend of the two angels who accompany each householder on its eve as he wends his way homeward from the synagogue; the conception that for its duration every devout Jew is possessed of an additional soul—an extra measure, so to speak, of spirituality; and all the other poetic notions, quaint or majestic, romantic or edifying, with which the myth-making capacity of a highly imaginative people could envelop a deeply loved institution.

A delight and medicament to the observant Jew, the Sabbath is also something more; it has ever been a restorative of the vigor of Judaism and the Jewish group—so potent a restorative that there is literal validity to the epigram of Ahad HaAm, modern philosopher of Judaism: "More than Israel has kept the Sabbath, the Sabbath has kept Israel."

*(Milton Steinberg)*

78

If the day is to have any dignity and significance, it must confront one of modern man's greatest curses, which is his internal and external unrest. This unrest arises from two principal sources: one, that he leads a life without goals and second, that he is involved in competition without end.

Shabbat is potentially an enormous relief from, and a protest against, these basic causes of unrest. Once a week it provides us with an opportunity to think about who we are; to deal not with the whatness of life, but the who-ness; not with things, but with persons; with creation and our part in it; with society and its needs; with ourselves as individuals and yet as social beings. If nothing happens to us during the Shabbat experience except an enlarging of our vision, we will have gained a new perspective of life's meaning and will have diminished our sense of unrest. That will be Shabbat rest in the sense required by our times: a protest against a life lived without goals.

Shabbat should be a surcease from and a protest against all forms of competition, even when they come in attractive packages marked self-advancement or self-improvement. I view the Sabbath in this respect as a "useless" day. We must once again understand that doing nothing, being silent and open to the world, letting things happen inside, can be as important as, and sometimes more important than, what we commonly call the useful. Let there be some special time during the week when we do for the sake of doing, when we love the trivial and, in fact, simply love; when we do for others rather than ourselves and thus provide a counterbalance for the weight of endless competition that burdens our every day.

*(W. Gunther Plaut)*

The eminence of the pause, the loftiness of silence was experienced, was discovered in this day. Nobility became a commandment and therefore communal, a nobility for everyone. There is no Sabbath which belongs only to an individual or to a few. As it is a people freely joined in labor, so this people is to become a people freely joined in rest, united in its rest. There is—taking the two words in their true sense—scarcely anything which is as aristocratic and as democratic at the same time as the Sabbath.

The Sabbath does not mean a mere not working, nor an empty idleness. It connotes something positive. It has guided the soul unto its mystery, so that it is not a day that just interrupts, but a day that renews, speaks through it, of something eternal. It is the expression of a direction for life and not just an instituted day of rest. If it were only that, or if it became that, its essence would be taken from it. It would then be only a hollow shell.

*(Leo Baeck)*

# GUIDE TO WEEKLY TORAH
# AND HAFTARAH READINGS

Each Shabbat has a special name which is usually taken from an opening or key word of the weekly Torah reading.

Alternative selections are provided on the principle of a triennial completion of reading the entire Torah. During the first year, follow selection (*a*), the second year ( *b*), the third year (*c*)—then begin again. It is suggested that a regular time be set aside on Shabbat to read the biblical texts. The following list is taken from the *Union Prayer Book*.

| TORAH | | HAFTARAH |
|---|---|---|
| *Bereshit* | | |
| (a) Genesis | I, 1—II, 3 | Isaiah XLII, 5-12 |
| (b) | II, 4-25 or | Psalm CIV or |
| | III, 1-24 | Job XXXVIII |
| (c) | IV, 1-16 | Psalm CXXXIX |
| *Noach* | | |
| (a) Genesis | VI, 9—VII, 7 | Isaiah LIV, 1-10 |
| (b) | VIII or IX | Jeremiah XXXI, 23-36 |
| (c) | XI, 1-9 | Zephaniah III, 8-20 |
| *Lech Lecha* | | |
| (a) Genesis | XII, 1-9 | Isaiah XL, 27—XLI, 10 |
| (b) | XIII or XIV | Isaiah LI, 1-16 or |
| | | Psalm CXI |
| (c) | XV | Psalm CV, 1-15 |
| *Vayera* | | |
| (a) Genesis | XVIII, 1-19 | II Kings IV, 8-37 |
| (b) | XVIII, 20-33 | Ezekiel XVIII |
| (c) | XXI or XXII | Micah VI, 1-8 |
| *Chayye Sarah* | | |
| (a) Genesis | XXIII | I Kings I, 5-36 |
| (b) | XXIV, 1-33 | Psalm XLV |
| (c) | XXIV, 34-67 | Proverbs XXXI, 10-31 |
| *Toledot* | | |
| (a) Genesis | XXV, 19-34 | Malachi I, 1-11 |
| (b) | XXVI, 12-33 | I Kings V, 15-26 |
| (c) | XXVII, 1-29 | Proverbs IV, 1-23 |
| *Vayetse* | | |
| (a) Genesis | XXVIII, 10-22 | Hosea XI, 7—XII, 11 |
| (b) | XXIX, 2-20 | Jeremiah XXXI, 1-17 |
| (c) | XXXI, 36-49 | Psalm XXVII |
| *Vayishlach* | | |
| (a) Genesis | XXXII, 4-33 | Hosea XII, 13—XIV, 3 |
| (b) | XXXIII | Psalm VII |
| (c) | XXXV, 1-20 | Jeremiah V, 1-16 |

| TORAH | | HAFTARAH |
|---|---|---|
| *Vayeshev* | | |
| (a) Genesis | XXXVII, 1-11 | I Kings III, 5-15 |
| (b) | XXXVII, 12-36 | Amos II, 6—III, 8 |
| (c) | XL | Psalm XXXIV |
| *Mikets* | | |
| (a) Genesis | XLI, 1-14 | I Kings III, 15-28 |
| (b) | XLI, 14-38 | Daniel II, 1-23 |
| (c) | XLII, 1-21 | Isaiah XIX, 11-15 |
| *Vayiggash* | | |
| (a) Genesis | XLIV, 18— | Ezekiel XXXVII, 15-28 |
| | XLV, 9 | |
| (b) | XLV, 9-28 | Psalm LXXII |
| (c) | XLVII, 1-12 | Psalm LXXI |
| *Vayechi* | | |
| (a) Genesis | XLVII, 28— | I Kings I, 41-53, II, 1-4 |
| | XLVIII, 20 | |
| (b) | XLIX, 1-28 | I Chronicles XXVIII, 1-10 |
| (c) | XLIX, 29— | Job V |
| | L, 26 | |
| *Shemot* | | |
| (a) Exodus | I, 1-22 | Isaiah XXVII, 6-8, 12— |
| | | XXVIII, 6 |
| (b) | II or III, 1-15 | Isaiah VI or I Samuel III |
| (c) | IV, 1-18 or V | Jeremiah I, 1-12 or |
| | | I Kings XII, 1-19 |
| *Va'era* | | |
| (a) Exodus | VI, 2-13 | Ezekiel XXVIII, 25— |
| | | XXIX, 16 |
| (b) | VII, 14-26 | Isaiah XLII, 5-17 |
| (c) | IX, 13-35 | Ezekiel XXXI, 1-12 |
| *Bo* | | |
| (a) Exodus | X, 1-23 | Jeremiah XLVI, 13-27 |
| (b) | XII, 1-11 | Ezra VI, 16-22 |
| (c) | XIII, 3-16 | Psalm CV, 14-45 |

| TORAH | | | HAFTARAH |
|---|---|---|---|
| *Beshallach* | | | |
| (a) Exodus | XIII, 17— | | Judges IV, 1-15 |
| | XIV, 15 | | |
| (b) | XV | | Judges V, 1-21 |
| (c) | XVI, 1-18 | | Psalm LXXVIII, 1-28 |
| *Yitro* | | | |
| (a) Exodus | XVIII | | Isaiah VI |
| (b) | XIX | | Isaiah XLIII, 1-12 |
| (c) | XX | | Psalm XIX |
| *Mishpatim* | | | |
| (a) Exodus | XXI, 1-13 | | Jeremiah XXXIV, 8-22; |
| | | | XXXIII, 25-26 |
| (b) | XXII, 20— | | Amos V, 6-24 |
| | XXIII, 9 | | |
| (c) | XXIV | | Jeremiah XVI, 19— |
| | | | XVII, 8 |
| *Terumah* | | | |
| (a) Exodus | XXV, 1-22 | | I Kings V, 26; VI, 13 |
| (b) | XXV, 23-40 | | I Chronicles XXII, 1-13 |
| (c) | XXVII, 1-19 | | I Kings VIII, 22-43 |
| *Tetsaveh* | | | |
| (a) Exodus | XXVII, 20— | | Ezekiel XLIII, 10-27 |
| | XXVIII, 12 | | |
| (b) | XXIX, 1-9 | | Isaiah LXI |
| (c) | XXIX, 38— | | Isaiah LXV, 17— |
| | XXX, 10 | | LXVI, 2 |
| *Ki Tisa* | | | |
| (a) Exodus | XXX, 11-31 | | I Kings XVIII, 20-39 |
| (b) | XXXII, 1-14 | | Psalm CVI, 1-23 |
| (c) | XXXIII, 12— | | Psalm LXXXI |
| | XXXIV, 10 | | |
| *Vayakhel* | | | |
| (a) Exodus | XXXV, 1-29 | | I Kings V, 9-26 |
| (b) | XXXV, 30— | | I Chronicles XXIX, 9-20 |
| | XXXVI, 7 | | |
| (c) | XXXVIII, 1-19 | | II Chronicles IV-V, 1 |

| TORAH | | HAFTARAH |
|---|---|---|
| *Pikude* | | |
| (a) Exodus | XXXVIII, 21—<br>XXXIX, 1 | I Kings VII, 1-14 |
| (b) | XXXIX, 32-43 | I Kings VIII, 10-30 |
| (c) | XL, 22-38 | I Kings VIII, 54-61 |
| *Vayikra* | | |
| (a) Leviticus | I | Isaiah XLIII, 21—<br>XLIV, 5 |
| (b) | II | Psalm L |
| (c) | V, 14-26 | Malachi II, 1-10 |
| *Tsav* | | |
| (a) Leviticus | VI, 1-11 | Jeremiah VII, 21-34 and<br>IX, 22-23 |
| (b) | VII, 22-38 | Hosea VI, 1-6 |
| (c) | VIII, 1-15 | Psalm CXXXII |
| *Shemini* | | |
| (a) Leviticus | IX, 1-16 | I Chronicles XVII |
| (b) | X, 1-11 | II Samuel VI, 1-19 |
| (c) | X, 12-19 | I Chronicles XV, 1-16 |
| *Tazria-Metsora* | | |
| (a) Leviticus | XII | II Kings V, 1-19 |
| (b) | XIV, 1-32 | Psalm XXXIV |
| (c) | XIV, 33-57 | Job II |
| *Achare Mot* | | |
| (a) Leviticus | XVI, 1-17 | Amos IX, 7-15 |
| (b) | XVI, 18-34 | Isaiah LIX |
| (c) | XVIII, 1-5;<br>24-30 | Ezekiel XXII, 17-30 |
| *Kedoshim* | | |
| (a) Leviticus | XIX, 1-14 | Ezekiel XXII, 1-15 |
| (b) | XIX, 23-37 | Psalm XV |
| (c) | XX, 22-27 | Job XXIX |
| *Emor* | | |
| (a) Leviticus | XXI, 1-8 | Ezekiel XLIV, 15-31 |
| (b) | XXII, 17-33 | Ezekiel XXXVI, 16-38 |
| (c) | XXIII, 1-8;<br>23-38 | Nehemiah VIII |

| TORAH | | | HAFTARAH |
|---|---|---|---|
| *Behar* | | | |
| (a) Leviticus | XXV, 1-13 | | Jeremiah XXXII, 6-27 |
| (b) | XXV, 14-34 | | Nehemiah V, 1-13 |
| (c) | XXV, 35-55 | | Zephaniah III |
| *Bechukotai* | | | |
| (a) Leviticus | XXVI, 3-13 | | Jeremiah XVI, 19— XVII, 14 |
| (b) | XXVI, 36-46 | | Job XXXVI, 3-26 |
| (c) | XXVII, 14-24 | | Psalm CXVI |
| *Bemidbar* | | | |
| (a) Numbers | I, 1-19 | | Hosea II, 1-3; 18-22 |
| (b) | II, 1-17 | | Psalm XX |
| (c) | III, 44-51 | | I Chronicles VI, 49-66 |
| *Naso* | | | |
| (a) Numbers | IV, 21-37 | | Judges XIII |
| (b) | VI, 1-17 | | Judges XVI, 4-21 |
| (c) | VI, 22-27 | | Psalm LXVII |
| *Beha'alotecha* | | | |
| (a) Numbers | VIII, 1-14 | | Zechariah II, 14—IV, 7 |
| (b) | X, 29—XI, 23 | | Psalm LXXVII |
| (c) | XI, 24—XII, 8 | | Joel II, 21—III, 5 |
| *Shelach Lecha* | | | |
| (a) Numbers | XIII | | Joshua II |
| (b) | XIV | | Joshua XIV, 6-14 |
| (c) | XIV, 26-45 | | Psalm CVI, 1-27; 44-48 |
| *Korach* | | | |
| (a) Numbers | XVI | | I Samuel XI, 14-16; XII, 1-8, 19-25 |
| (b) | XVII, 16-24 | | Isaiah LVI, 1-8 |
| (c) | XVIII, 1-20 | | Jeremiah V, 20-31 |
| *Chukat* | | | |
| (a) Numbers | XIX, 1-10 | | Ezekiel XXXVI, 21-38 |
| (b) | XX, 1-21 | | Judges XI, 4-33 |
| (c) | XXI, 1-20 | | Psalm XLII |

|  TORAH | | | HAFTARAH |
| --- | --- | --- | --- |

*Balak*

| (a) Numbers | XXII, 2-20 | Micah V, 6-14; VI, 1-8 |
| --- | --- | --- |
| (b) | XXIII, 5-26 | Isaiah LIV, 11-17 |
| (c) | XXIV, 1-18 | Habakkuk, III |

*Pinchas*

| (a) Numbers | XXV, 10-18 | I Kings XIX |
| --- | --- | --- |
| (b) | XXVII, 1-11 | Judges I, 1-15 |
| (c) | XXVII, 12-23 | Joshua XXIII, 1-15 |

*Matot*

| (a) Numbers | XXX, 2-17 | Jeremiah I, 1-14 |
| --- | --- | --- |
| (b) | XXXII, 1-19 | Joshua XXII, 1-10 |
| (c) | XXXII, 20-32 | Joshua XXII, 11-34 |

*Mas'e*

| (a) Numbers | XXXIII, 1-10 | Jeremiah II, 4-13 |
| --- | --- | --- |
| (b) | XXXV, 9-34 | Joshua XX |
| (c) | XXXVI | Jeremiah XXXIII, 1-16; 25-27 |

*Devarim*

| (a) Deuteronomy I, 1-17 | Isaiah I, 1-27 |
| --- | --- |
| (b) | II, 1-9 | Jeremiah IX, 9-23 |
| (c) | III, 1-14 | Lamentations III, 19-41 |

*Vaetchanan*

| (a) Deuteronomy III, 23—IV, 8 | Isaiah XL, 1-26 |
| --- | --- |
| (b) | V | Psalm CIII |
| (c) | VI | Zechariah VIII, 7-23 |

*Ekev*

| (a) Deuteronomy VII, 12-21 | Isaiah XLIX, 14-26 |
| --- | --- |
| (b) | VIII | Isaiah I, 1-10 |
| (c) | X, 12—XI, 12 | I Chronicles XXIX, 10-20 |

*Re'eh*

| (a) Deuteronomy XI, 26-32 | Isaiah LIV, II—LV, 5 |
| --- | --- |
| (b) | XIV, 1-8, 22-29 | Psalm XXIV |
| (c) | XV, 1-18 | Isaiah XXVI, 1-12 |

| TORAH | HAFTARAH |
|---|---|

**Shoftim**
| | | |
|---|---|---|
| (a) Deuteronomy XVI, 18—XVII, 14 | | Isaiah LI, 12—LII, 6 |
| (b) | XVIII, 9-22 | Jeremiah XXIII, 16-32 |
| (c) | XXI, 1-9 | Ezekiel XXXIV, 1-24 |

**Ki Tetse**
| | | |
|---|---|---|
| (a) Deuteronomy XXI, 10-14 | | Isaiah LIV, 1-10 |
| (b) | XXII, 1-10 | Proverbs XXX, 1-9 |
| (c) | XXIV, 10-24 | Isaiah V, 1-16 |

**Ki Tavo**
| | | |
|---|---|---|
| (a) Deuteronomy XXVI, 1-15 | | Isaiah LX |
| (b) | XXVII, 1-10 | Joshua IV |
| (c) | XXVIII, 1-14 | Isaiah XXXV |

**Nitsavim**
| | | |
|---|---|---|
| (a) Deuteronomy XXIX, 9-28 | | Isaiah LXI, 10—LXII |
| (b) | XXX, 1-10 | Isaiah LI, 1-16 |
| (c) | XXX, 11-20 | Psalm LXXIII |

**Vayelech**
| | | |
|---|---|---|
| (a) Deuteronomy XXXI, 1-13 | | Hosea XIV, 2-10 (see note) |
| (b) | XXXI, 14-21 | Ibid |
| (c) | XXXI, 22-30 | Ibid |

**Ha'azinu**
| | | |
|---|---|---|
| (a) Deuteronomy XXXII, 1-12 | | II Samuel XXII, 1-32 (see note) |
| (b) | XXXII, 13-29 | Psalm XVIII, 1-21 |
| (c) | XXXII, 30-52 | Psalm XVIII, 22-51 |

**Vezot Haberachah**
| | | |
|---|---|---|
| (a) Deuteronomy XXXIII, 1-17 | | Joshua I |
| (b) | XXXIII, 18-19 | Ibid. |
| (c) | XXXIV | Ibid. |

*Note:* Hosea XIV is the Haftarah either for Vayelech or Ha'azinu, depending upon which one falls on Shabbat Shuvah. If Vayelech is not on Shabbat Shuvah then it is combined with Nitsavim, in which case read the Haftarah indicated for Nitsavim. If Ha'azinu is not on Shabbat Shuvah read the Haftarah indicated above.

# SPECIAL READINGS

| | TORAH | HAFTARAH |
|---|---|---|
| Pesach, first day | Exodus XII, 37-42; XIII, 3-10 | Isaiah XLIII, 1-15 |
| Pesach, seventh day | Exodus XIV, 30 XV, 21 | Isaiah XL, 1-6, 9, XII |
| Shavuot | Exodus XIX, 1-8; XX, 1-18 | Isaiah XLII, 1-12 |
| Succot, first day | Leviticus XXIII, 33-44 | Is. XXXII—XXXIII—XXXV |
| Shemini Atseret | Deuteronomy XXXIV and Genesis I, 1-10 | Joshua I, 1-17 |
| For the first Shabbat of Hanukkah | Weekly Torah Portion | Zechariah IV, 1-7 |
| For the second Shabbat of Hanukkah | Weekly Torah Portion | I Kings VIII, 54-66 |
| For the Shabbat preceding Purim (Zachor) | Weekly Torah Portion | Esther VII, 1-10; VIII, 15-17; or IX, 20-28 |
| For Shabbat preceding Pesach (Hagadol) | Weekly Torah Portion | Malachi III, 4-24 |
| For the Shabbat during Pesach | Exodus XXXIII, 12—XXXIV, 26 | Song of Songs, II, 7-17; or Ezekiel XXXVII, 1-15 |
| For the Shabbat during Succot | Exodus XXXIII, 12—XXXIV, 26 | Ecclesiastes I, V, VII, VIII or XII or Ezekiel XXXIX, 1-16 |

# QUESTIONS AND ANSWERS
# ABOUT SHABBAT

## Q. Who should light Shabbat candles?

**A.** Rabbi Solomon B. Freehof responds: There are many households in which the mother has died and an unmarried daughter kindles the Sabbath lights. I have seen no law or hint of a custom to the effect that an unmarried daughter may not kindle the Sabbath lights . . . The duty of lighting the Sabbath lights rests primarily, but not exclusively, upon women. The Mishnah (Shabbat 11:6) counts this as one of the three commandments especially enjoined upon women. The Shulchan Aruch (Orach Hayyim 263:3) states the law clearly and explains it as follows: "Women are especially commanded as to the Sabbath lights because they are at home and tend to household matters."

However, it is made clear (in #2) that both men and women are enjoined to make sure that the lights are kindled. The primary duty rests upon the women. Nevertheless, travelers and students are expected to light the lights in their lodging places (#6). The law, then, is that both sexes share in the obligation to be sure that the lights are lit. The woman should light them, but if she is ill the man may do so. If the man is away from home he must light them where he lodges.

## Q. What is the proper hour for lighting Shabbat candles?

**A.** According to tradition, the lighting of Shabbat candles is a mitzvah, but Scripture expressly prohibits the kindling of fire in any form once Shabbat has begun. Hence it became obligatory to light Shabbat candles before sunset on Friday. As the hour of sunset varies with the change of the seasons, so does the time for lighting the candles. Candle-light time is indicated throughout the year in most Hebrew calendars and it may be as early as 4:10 o'clock in the winter or as late as 8:10 o'clock in the summer in northern climes.

In homes where lighting of Shabbat candles is observed in accordance with the changing hour of sunset, the candle lighting and the Shabbat meal are unrelated to each other. However, in many liberal Jewish homes it has become the custom to have the Shabbat eve meal preceded immediately by the candle-lighting ceremony. Under such circumstances, the candles are lit at the same time every Friday night in the year, which means that in the winter time they will be lit after sunset and in the summer months before sunset. Reform Judaism considers both methods correct and proper though, to be sure, it recognizes that the latter method disregards the traditional law against kindling a fire on the Shabbat.

In a large number of Reform congregations, it is the practice to have the candle-lighting ceremony take place in the synagogue at the beginning of the Shabbat eve service which generally occurs after sundown. A woman of the congregation lights the candles and recites the traditional blessing over them. In other congregations, the same ceremony is observed, but regard is given to the prohibition against kindling fire on the Shabbat and the candles, therefore, are lit before the service begins. In still other congregations the candle lighting ceremony is avoided altogether.

**Q. Why do Reform Congregations conduct their Friday night services at a late hour? Is this not contrary to Jewish tradition?**

**A.** According to talmudic principle, the afternoon (Minchah) prayers may be recited at any hour between noon and sunset, and the evening (Ma'ariv) prayers at any hour between sunset and midnight. For the sake of economy of time, Orthodox congregations, as a rule, schedule the afternoon worship so that it occurs immediately before sunset and the evening worship so that it occurs immediately after sunset. The worshipper is thus enabled to participate in both the afternoon and evening services through a single visit to the synagogue. This practice is followed on weekdays and holidays as well as on Shabbat. Because the hour of sunset undergoes seasonal changes, both afternoon and evening services in Orthodox synagogues follow an ever-changing time schedule throughout the year.

The late Shabbat eve services were instituted by Reform congregations in order to establish a fixed hour for worship every Friday night in the year. Even from an Orthodox viewpoint, there can be no objection to this. The practical advantage of holding services at a fixed hour is such that the practice has spread to most Conservative congregations and even to some that consider themselves Orthodox.

**Q. Is the public reading of the Torah at Friday night services in Reform Congregations a violation of Jewish tradition?**

**A.** Traditionally, the public reading of the Torah always occurred at the Shabbat morning service; it was not read at the Friday night service. However, the practice of Reform congregations in reading the Torah at the evening service, while contrary to tradition, in no way violates Jewish law. Scripture says of the Torah, "Thou shalt meditate therein day and night." From any Jewish point of view, there can be no possible objection to having the Torah read publicly at a Shabbat eve service (although traditional law would require that it also be read on Shabbat morning).

Practical considerations are responsible for this innovation. Many Jews find it difficult, or even impossible, to attend the Shabbat morning services, and are thus deprived of the mitzvah of hearing the Torah read. It was for their sake that the practice of reading the Torah at the Friday night service was instituted.

In those congregations which follow the practice of reading the Torah at the Shabbat eve service, it is natural and normal for Bar Mitzvah and Bat Mitzvah celebrations to occur during the evening worship.

**Q. Did the Reform movement at one time contemplate giving up the Shabbat in favor of Sunday worship?**

**A.** At no time did the Reform movement consider giving up the Shabbat. In the earlier part of the century, a goodly number of Reform congregations conducted Sunday morning services as *supplementary* to their Shabbat worship. Economic conditions made it impossible for most members of these congregations to attend Shabbat services, and the Sunday morning worship was instituted to enable them to be in the synagogue on a day when they were not engaged in business. It is true that in some of these congregations the attendance on Sunday morning was greater than it was on Shabbat. Only one Reform congregation, to our knowledge, abandoned Shabbat worship altogether in favor of the Sunday service. Today, only a handful of Reform congregations continue to hold a major service on Sunday morning, but all conduct services on Shabbat.

**Q. Why are weddings not permitted on Shabbat?**

**A.** Talmudic law (Betsah 36b, 37a) states that one may not betroth a wife on Shabbat as a preventive measure lest one write a betrothal or marriage contract. The writings of such contracts is prohibited on Shabbat. A further reason for avoiding weddings on Shabbat is based on the principle that one does not confuse one joyous occasion with another *(En me'arvin simchah besimchah)*, Shabbat being one joyous occasion and a wedding another. On the basis of this principle, weddings are prohibited on all holy days.

**Q. Why do Reform Congregations permit blowing the Shofar on a Rosh Hashanah which falls on a Shabbat, while Orthodox Congregations do not?**

**A.** The following answer was given by Rabbi Jacob Z. Lauterbach in 1923: There is no reason why the shofar should not be blown on a Rosh Hashanah which falls on a Saturday in congregations where only one day of Rosh Hashanah is observed. During Temple times the distinction was made between the Temple in Jerusalem and the Synagogues in the provinces, in that only in the former was the shofar blown on a Saturday. After the Temple was destroyed, R. Johanan b. Zakkai instituted the practice that wherever there is a Beth Din, that is, a rabbinical tribunal, the shofar should be blown on Saturday (Mishnah, Rosh Hashanah IV:1).

Commenting on this Mishnah, the Babylonian Gemara (R.H. 29b) declares that blowing of the shofar is an art but not work and hence by biblical law is permitted on Saturday, but that rabbinical law prohibits it on Saturday for the reason lest it might happen that the one who is to perform the ceremony would wish to go to an expert in order to practice, and thus carry the shofar with him on the Sabbath day, which act, that is, the carrying of it, is prohibited on the Sabbath. . . .

Some of the rabbinical authorities rightly say, on the same ground one could argue that the ceremony should be altogether prohibited, even on Rosh Hashanah falling on a weekday for fear . . . that the Shofar might need repairing and this will lead to doing work which is prohibited on a holiday. Of course, they answer that in this case the fear lest it might lead to the sin of doing repair work on Yom Tov is not to be entertained for it would have the result of entirely abolishing the ceremony. This latter argument is quite correct and it applies with equal force to the question of blowing the shofar on Rosh Hashanah which falls on a Sabbath day in those congregations where only one day of Rosh Hashanah is observed, for if we allow the consideration, lest the shofar might be carried on the street, to interfere with the performance of the ceremony, the result will be that, for that year at least, the ceremony will be entirely omitted and we should not abolish this characteristic ceremony, even for one year.

**Q.** **Catering for a Bar Mitzvah reception following a Shabbat service has become a commonplace feature of present-day Jewish life. Kosher caterers who come into the Synagogue will deliver and prepare the food before Shabbat begins. What position should we take with respect to other caterers who deliver the food on Shabbat and prepare it in the Synagogue kitchen?**

**A.** The following answer was given by Rabbi Solomon B. Freehof in 1963: This question, also, touches an unsolved larger problem in the relationship between Reform and the legal tradition. How strict should we be in Sabbath observance? We have to go by our feelings in the matter. We certainly would not ask a Jewish caterer to work for us on the Sabbath, nor would we make an arrangement with a Gentile caterer, asking him specifically to come on the Sabbath and work. We simply ask him to cater the Bar Mitzvah. The day which he picks for his preparatory work is his choice. We are paying him for the job. All this would be strictly in the line of Jewish law with regard to Gentile employment.

But this, also, happening in the synagogue, makes a difference. According to the law, even the general contract permitting a Christian to work on his own time would not be permitted if the work is done on a Jewish street, because it would look as if the Jew commanded the work to be done on the Sabbath, and we are concerned with the look of things (mar'ith ayin, *i.e.,* with the impression it makes on the public). We must therefore decide this matter of whether we can have a Christian caterer work on the Sabbath preparing food, on the impression it would make on the congregation. I think there are some congregations that might not mind it. I think that most would be unfavorably impressed, for the sake of mar'ith ayin. If the congregation would not object to it, I do not think the rabbi should raise an objection. But as a contrast, the Gift Corner, which is run by Jews and involves buying and selling on the congregation premises, should not be permitted to be open on the Sabbath.

**Q. Is it permissible to let a non-Jewish contractor, building a Synagogue, work on the building on Shabbat?**

**A.** The following answer was given by Rabbi Jacob Z. Lauterbach in 1927: Jewish religious law forbids Jews to do any work on the Sabbath or to have his servant or agent do it for him. The Jew is, therefore, not allowed to hire laborers to do work for him on the Sabbath. He may, however, let out work to a non-Jew and need not concern himself whether the non-Jew does it on Sabbath or not, provided that the non-Jew has the time and could if he would do the work on weekdays. . . .

There is only one consideration that might keep the Jew from letting the non-Jew do any work for him on the Sabbath, even when the work is contracted for. This is the consideration lest other Jews, seeing the non-Jew doing the Jewish work on the Sabbath and not knowing that it was contracted for, might suspect the Jew of letting his hired laborer or agent work for him on Sabbath. This might lead to laxity in the observance of the Sabbath on the part of other Jews. To avoid suspicion, the Jew should not let a non-Jew work for him on Sabbath even by contract when conditions are such as to cause other people to think that the Jew for whom the work is done is violating the Sabbath. . . .

Rabbi Abraham Abele Gumbiner, a gerat Polish rabbinical authority (1635-1683), in his commentary Magen Avraham to Shulchan Aruch, Orach Chayyim 244:8, therefore, says that a community should be allowed to have a synagogue built by non-Jews on the Sabbath, if the work is done by contract.

Solomon Jehudah Rappaport in his responsum published in his Beth Talmud also hesitates to forbid a synagogue to be built on the Sabbath by non-Jews. After a rather lengthy discussion he finally arrives at the following decision: If there is an absolute need of the new Temple, it is to be permitted. If, however, there is no absolute need for it, *i.e.,* if the congregation has a house of worship, but merely wants to have a better, more convenient, and more beautiful Temple, then we should first make all efforts to arrange with the contractors, even at the risk of additional expense, that they do not work on it on the Sabbath. If this cannot be done, at least let no one, representing the congregation, be seen there on the Sabbath supervising the work or watching the laborers.

I think that this decision of Rappaport should be followed. Since it is a matter of sentiment more than of Law, all efforts should be made to arrange, if possible, not to have the work done on the Sabbath, even if it should involve extra outlay on the part of the congregation. I make this decision with great hesitancy because my sentiments are against giving the permission, but I must in truth state that the Law does not offer any serious objection to it.

**Q. What position does Reform Judaism take with respect to biblical and talmudic prohibitions against doing work or engaging in business on Shabbat?**

**A.** While Reform Judaism has great respect for biblical and talmudic law and for those halachah-conscious Jews who observe the Shabbat in all its minutiae, it recognizes the realities of modern life and the difficulties and hardships many Jews would encounter if they attempted to fulfill all the requirements of Shabbat observance. Reform Judaism is no less conscious of the sanctity of the Shabbat than is traditional Judaism, but has taken the view that those aspects of Shabbat observance that are capable of fulfillment and which enrich spiritually both the individual and the community should be given greater emphasis than some laws which many Jews find impossible to carry out because of economic pressures.

Both biblical and rabbinic law prohibit one from performing manual labor in any form or engaging in any kind of business on Shabbat. The realities of modern economic life make it difficult, if not impossible, for many Jews to honor these prohibitions. Many Jews are employed by non-Jewish business establishments which require them to work on Shabbat. The competitive aspects of the business, industrial, and professional world compel other Jews to engage in labor or commerce on the seventh day or else suffer economic ruin. In numerous instances, Jews own or manage businesses which employ non-Jews who are not committed to Shabbat observance and who would be greatly disadvantaged economically if forced to observe the seventh day as a day of rest. Nevertheless, while recognizing that forces beyond the individual's control may prevent some Jews from keeping Shabbat as a day of rest, Reform Judaism still upholds the principle that proper Shabbat observance calls for cessation from unnecessary work and business activity.

If one is not normally engaged in work or business on Shabbat, or if the nature of his business is such that he is not required to work on Shabbat, it would be improper for him to engage in work or business on the seventh day. One should also abstain from all heavy housework such as laundering, ironing, and general house cleaning. However, it is not improper on the Sabbath to perform such lighter household tasks as washing dishes and pots and pans used for Shabbat meals, making beds, setting the table, or keeping a room tidy and neat, nor do we consider it improper to pursue one's personal hobby designed for Oneg Shabbat.

On Shabbat one should avoid marketing or shopping for food, apparel, furniture, or any other items which can be purchased on other days of the week. It is not improper to purchase medicines or other needs for someone who has fallen ill. One should also avoid renting or buying a home, purchasing an automobile or signing contracts for such transactions. The general rule is that one should not in any way violate the prohibitions against work and business on Shabbat when there is no necessity for such violation. If emergency repairs are necessary to avoid possible hazards, it is not improper on Shabbat to do whatever work is necessary to remove the hazard. For example, if there is a short in the electrical wiring which may cause fire to break out, or a leak in the plumbing

which will do extensive damage in a home, one need not post-
pone taking care of these matters until after Shabbat is over;
one may tend to them immediately. As one is obligated to
break any Shabbat rule in order to help one who is sick, so,
in the view of Reform Judaism, should one be willing to do
whatever work is necessary on Shabbat to · remove an im-
mediate hazard.

# GLOSSARY

Throughout this Shabbat Manual, some key words have been used in Hebrew. This Glossary translates and interprets these terms.

*Avodah:* "Worship."

*Bar Mitzvah:* "Son of mitzvah" (original meaning: obligated to do mitzvah); status of the thirteen-year-old boy who undertakes performance of the mitzvot by himself.

*Bat Mitzvah:* "Daughter of mitzvah"; status of the thirteen-year-old girl who undertakes performance of the mitzvot by herself.

*Birkat Hamazon:* "Blessing of the meal"; prayer said after eating.

*Berit:* "Covenant"; distinctive relationship of the people of Israel with God.

*Challah:* "Bread loaf"; name given to special Shabbat bread used for saying motzi at the beginning of Shabbat or holiday meal.

*Erev Shabbat:* "Eve of Sabbath"; Friday.

*Gemilut Chasadim:* "Acts of loving concern"; according to the Sages, one of the three fundamentals of human obligation and opportunity.

*Haftarah:* "Conclusion"; biblical reading in addition to Torah portion.

*Havdalah:* "Separation"; prayers and ritual concluding Shabbat.

*Halachah:* "Way to go"; Jewish law.

*Kedushah:* "Holiness"; the Hebrew word has the connotation of "separation," "setting aside."

*Kiddush:* "Sanctification"; prayers said usually over wine to signify the beginning of Shabbat or holiday.

*Minchah:* "Afternoon"; afternoon prayers.

*Mitzvah* (plural, *mitzvot*): "Commandment"; performance of an act of distinctive Jewish quality often accompanied by a blessing.

*Menuchah:* "Rest."

*Motzi:* "He who brings forth"; key word in the blessing over food; said before eating.

*Oneg:* "Joy."

*Oneg Shabbat:* "Joy of the sabbath"; often also used for collation after Shabbat services.

*Shabbat:* "Sabbath," the seventh day of the week.

*Shabbat Menuchah:* "Sabbath rest"; condition of repose on Shabbat.

*Shabbat Shalom:* "Sabbath peace"; greeting for Shabbat.

*Shacharit:* "Morning"; morning prayers.

*Shemirat Shabbat:* "Observance of the Sabbath."

*Sidra:* "Arrangement"; term for weekly Torah portion.

*Torah:* "Instruction"; Five Books of Moses; in a wider sense, the whole range of Jewish learning.

*Zemirot:* "Songs"; special hymns sung on Shabbat.

# ACKNOWLEDGMENTS

Grateful acknowledgment is made to the following publishers who have granted permission for use of material copyrighted by them.

B'NAI B'RITH: Abraham Isaac Kuk, in *Contemporary Jewish Thought, Great Books Series* Vol. 4 (Washington, 1963) p. 108 f.

EAST AND WEST LIBRARY: Martin Buber, *Moses* (Oxford, 1947), p. 82.

FARRAR, STRAUS & GIROUX: Robert Gordis, *Judaism for the Modern Age* (New York, 1955), p. 174. Abraham J. Heschel, *The Sabbath* (New York, 1961), pp. 6 ff.

HARCOURT, BRACE & WORLD: Milton Steinberg, *Basic Judaism* (New York, 1947), p. 129 f.

HEBREW UNION COLLEGE PRESS: Jacob Z. Lauterbach, *Rabbinic Essays* (Cincinnati, 1951), p. 411. Solomon B. Freehof, *Reform Responsa* (Cincinnati, 1960), pp. 24 ff.

HOLT, RINEHART & WINSTON: Leo Baeck, *This People Israel* (New York, 1965), p. 136 f.

JONATHAN DAVID PUBLISHERS: Eliezer Berkovits, *God, Man and History* (2nd ed., New York, 1945) p. 123f.

SCHOCKEN BOOKS: Franz Rosenzweig, *His Life and Thought,* edited by Nahum N. Glatzer (Philadelphia, 1956), p. 245f.

UNION OF AMERICAN HEBREW CONGREGATIONS: Samuel S. Cohon, *Judaism as a Way of Life* (New York, 1948), p. 261f.

# MUSIC ACKNOWLEDGMENTS

Every effort has been made to ascertain the owners of copyrights for the music used in this volume. The Central Conference of American Rabbis expresses its gratitude to those whose names as composers, arrangers, or publishers appear below for permission to use the compositions indicated.

We are grateful to Cantor Arthur Wolfson of New York, Cantor Lawrence Avery of New Rochelle, New York and Mr. Ben Steinberg of Toronto, for their assistance.

| *Composer and Arranger* | *Title* |
|---|---|
| A. W. Binder: | "Kindling the Shabbat Lights" © copyright 1940, Transcontinental Music Publications. |
| Shlomo Carlebach: | "V'haer Eyneynu" © copyright 1969 |
| M. Helfman: | "Birkat Hamazon Bik'tzarah" © copyright Brandeis Institute. |
| N. Hirsch: | "Oseh Shalom" © copyright 1970, Or-Tav Music Publications Tel-Aviv, Israel. |
| M. Nathanson: | "Shir Hamaalot"; Birkat Hamazon" © copyright 1954, Hebrew Publishing Company and Cantors Assembly of America "Yism'chu" © copyright 1934 Hebrew Publishing Company. |
| S. Secunda: | "Shabbat Shalom" from *Oneg Shabbat* © 1964, Mills Music Inc., reprinted by permission of Belwyn-Mills. |
| B. Steinberg: | "N'kadmah Fanav" © copyright 1964, Transcontinental Music Publications. |
| A. Yolkoff: | "Hayom Yom Shabbat" from *Shirat Atideinu* © copyright 1966, Transcontinental Music Publications. |
| D. Zahavi: | "Elee, Elee" from "Chof Kaisariah" © copyright Merkaz Letarbut Ulechinuch, Tel-Aviv, Israel. |
| M. Zeira: | "L'chah Dodee" © copyright 1960 Merkaz Letarbut Ulechinuch, Tel-Aviv, Israel. |